LEIPZIG TR.
GUIDE 20

**Your Essential Companion to Unveiling the
Soul of Saxony Best-Kept Secrets, Explore
Historical Landmarks, Experience Local
Culture, and Plan Your Perfect Trip**

Grace M. Smith

TABLE OF CONTENTS

INTRODUCTION

Leipzig captured my heart from the moment I stepped onto its cobblestone streets, each one whispering stories of centuries past. My journey began with a stroll through the historic city center, where ornate facades and charming alleyways led me on a captivating exploration of Leipzig's rich heritage.

One of the highlights of my trip was visiting the St. Thomas Church, where the legendary composer Johann Sebastian Bach once served as the music director. As I sat in the pews listening to a hauntingly beautiful organ performance, I couldn't help but feel a profound sense of reverence for the musical genius who once graced these hallowed halls.

Another unforgettable experience was ascending the steps of the Monument to the Battle of the Nations, a towering monument commemorating the pivotal Battle of Leipzig during the Napoleonic Wars. From the top, I gazed out over the sprawling cityscape, reflecting on the significance of this historic site and the bravery of those who fought here. But Leipzig isn't just a city steeped in history; it's also a vibrant hub of culture and creativity. I spent an enchanting evening at the Leipzig Opera House, where I was mesmerized by a spellbinding performance of Mozart's "The Magic Flute." The exquisite music, lavish sets, and stellar cast transported me to another world, leaving me utterly spellbound.

Of course, no trip to Leipzig would be complete without sampling the local cuisine. I indulged in hearty Saxon dishes at cozy taverns, sipped on aromatic coffee at bustling cafes, and treated myself to decadent pastries at artisan bakeries. Each bite was a culinary delight, tantalizing my taste buds and leaving me craving more.

But perhaps the most cherished memories of my time in Leipzig are the moments spent simply wandering its streets, soaking in the sights, sounds, and smells of this enchanting city. Whether strolling through leafy parks, browsing through bustling markets, or striking up conversations with friendly locals, every moment felt like a treasure to be savored. Leipzig may be a city of stone and mortar, but its true beauty lies in the warmth of its people, the richness of its culture, and the indelible mark it leaves on the hearts of all who visit.

LEIPZIG AND BEYOND
A SNAPSHOT OF THE REGION

Situated in the heart of Germany, the Leipzig region stands as a vibrant testament to the country's rich history, dynamic culture, and forward-thinking innovation. From its bustling city center to its picturesque countryside, the Leipzig region offers a diverse array of experiences that captivate visitors and residents alike.

Geography

Spanning the eastern part of the Free State of Saxony, the Leipzig region is characterized by its rolling hills, lush forests, and meandering rivers. At its center lies the city of Leipzig, a bustling metropolis renowned for its architectural splendor and cultural significance. Surrounding Leipzig are charming towns and villages, each with its own unique charm and character, contributing to the region's diverse landscapes.

To the west, the Leipzig region is bordered by the majestic River Elbe, while to the east, the Mulde River winds through the scenic countryside. This strategic location has not only shaped the region's physical landscape but has also played a crucial role in its economic development and cultural identity.

History

The roots of the Leipzig region can be traced back over a thousand years, with evidence of human settlement dating as far back as the Stone Age. Throughout its storied history, the region has been shaped by conquests, wars, and revolutions, each leaving its mark on the land and its people.

One of the most significant chapters in the region's history unfolded during the Middle Ages when Leipzig emerged as a prominent trade hub, thanks to its strategic location at the crossroads of important trade routes. The Leipzig Trade Fair, founded in the 12th century, played a pivotal role in shaping the city's fortunes, attracting merchants and traders from far and wide.

In more recent times, Leipzig has been a beacon of hope and resilience, particularly during the peaceful protests of 1989 that ultimately led to the fall of the Berlin Wall and the reunification of Germany. This momentous event, known as the Peaceful Revolution, cemented Leipzig's reputation as a symbol of freedom and democracy.

Culture and Heritage

The Leipzig region boasts a rich cultural heritage that is celebrated in its vibrant arts scene, historic landmarks, and festive traditions. At the heart of this cultural landscape is the city of Leipzig itself, home to world-renowned institutions such as the St. Thomas Church, where Johann Sebastian Bach once served as a cantor, and the Leipzig Opera House, which showcases performances ranging from classical masterpieces to contemporary works.

Throughout the year, the region comes alive with a myriad of cultural events and festivals, offering visitors the opportunity to immerse themselves in the local traditions and customs. From the Leipzig Bach Festival, which pays homage to the city's most famous resident, to the Leipzig Christmas Market, where the scent of mulled wine and roasted almonds fills the air, there is always something to see and do in the Leipzig region.

Economy and Innovation
In addition to its rich cultural heritage, the Leipzig region is also a thriving economic center, with a diverse range of industries driving its growth and prosperity. From automotive manufacturing to renewable energy, the region is home to a host of innovative companies and research institutions that are at the forefront of their respective fields.

One of the key drivers of the region's economy is the Leipzig/Halle Airport, one of the busiest cargo airports in Europe, facilitating trade and commerce on a global scale. Additionally, the Leipzig Trade Fair continues to play a vital role in connecting businesses from around the world, providing a platform for networking, collaboration, and growth. The Leipzig region is a vibrant and dynamic destination that offers something for everyone. Whether you're exploring the historic streets of Leipzig, immersing yourself in the region's rich cultural heritage, or engaging with its innovative industries, you're sure to be captivated by all that the Leipzig region has to offer. So come and discover the magic of this unique corner of Germany for yourself.

What Makes Leipzig Worth Visiting

People who have had the pleasure of experiencing Leipzig's charm will always have a particular place in their hearts for this city that is bursting with history, culture, and innovation. Leipzig has a lot to offer tourists from near and far, from a thriving cultural scene to ancient sites and gorgeous parks. These experiences are sure to enthrall and inspire travelers. Let me tell you about my own experience and why Leipzig is a unique place to visit.

1 A City Steeped in History

Stepping into Leipzig feels like taking a journey back in time. The city's cobblestone streets whisper tales of centuries past, from its medieval origins as a trading hub to its pivotal role in the events that shaped modern Europe. Walking through the historic city center, I was struck by the grandeur of landmarks like the St. Thomas Church, where Johann Sebastian Bach composed some of his most famous works, and the imposing Leipzig Gewandhaus, home to one of the world's oldest symphony orchestras.

2 Cultural Delights at Every Turn

Leipzig's cultural scene is as diverse as it is vibrant, offering something to suit every taste and interest. As an avid art enthusiast, I found myself drawn to the city's many galleries and museums, each offering a unique glimpse into Leipzig's rich cultural heritage. From the masterpieces of the New Leipzig School at the Museum der Bildenden Künste to the thought-provoking exhibits at the Zeitgeschichtliches Forum Leipzig, there was never a dull moment.

3 Music and Melodies in the Air

Music permeates every corner of Leipzig, earning it the title of "City of Music." As a lover of classical music, I was in awe of the city's musical legacy, from the legendary performances at the Leipzig Opera House to the stirring melodies of street musicians echoing through the streets. One of the highlights of my visit was attending a concert at the Leipzig Gewandhaus, where I was transported to another world by the breathtaking sound of the orchestra.

4 Green Spaces and Urban Oases

Despite its bustling city center, Leipzig is also blessed with an abundance of green spaces where visitors can escape the hustle and bustle of urban life. One of my favorite memories from my time in Leipzig was exploring the expansive Clara-Zetkin-Park, where lush meadows and tranquil lakes provided the perfect backdrop for a leisurely stroll or a relaxing picnic. The Leipzig Zoo was another highlight, offering the chance to get up close and personal with a wide range of exotic animals from around the world.

5 Culinary Delights and Gastronomic Adventures

No visit to Leipzig would be complete without indulging in its culinary delights. From hearty traditional dishes like Leipziger Allerlei to innovative fusion cuisine at trendy restaurants, Leipzig offers a culinary experience like no other. One of the highlights of my trip was sampling local delicacies at the bustling Leipzig Markt, where vendors offered everything from freshly baked bread to artisanal cheeses and locally sourced produce.

A Hub of Innovation and Creativity

Leipzig's spirit of innovation is palpable, with the city serving as a hub for groundbreaking research, technology, and entrepreneurship. As someone with a keen interest in innovation, I was fascinated by the city's thriving startup scene and its commitment to sustainability and social responsibility. Visiting the Leipzig Trade Fair was a highlight of my trip, providing insight into the latest trends and developments shaping industries ranging from automotive manufacturing to renewable energy.

Leipzig is a city that captivates the imagination and leaves a lasting impression on all who visit. Whether you're drawn to its rich history, vibrant culture, or spirit of innovation, Leipzig offers a wealth of experiences just waiting to be discovered. So why visit Leipzig? For the chance to embark on an unforgettable journey filled with adventure, discovery, and endless possibilities.

CHAPTER 1
CRAFTING YOUR LEIPZIG
ADVENTURE

In Crafting Your Leipzig Adventure, we'll delve into essential aspects of trip planning, including transportation options, accommodation choices, must-see attractions, dining recommendations, and tips for making the most of your time in Leipzig. Whether you're a first-time visitor or a seasoned traveler, these insights will help you create an unforgettable experience in this captivating city.

Finding the Perfect Time to Experience Leipzig

When to visit Leipzig is a question that often arises when planning a trip to this enchanting city. The truth is, Leipzig offers something special in every season, making it a destination worth visiting year-round. Let's explore the different times of the year and what they have to offer to help you decide when to embark on your Leipzig adventure.

1 Spring: Blossoming Beauty

Springtime in Leipzig is a sight to behold. As nature awakens from its winter slumber, the city bursts into life with colorful blooms and fresh greenery. One of the highlights of visiting Leipzig in spring is exploring its numerous parks and gardens, such as the idyllic Clara-Zetkin-Park or the botanical wonders of the Leipzig Botanical Garden. The city's outdoor cafes and beer gardens also come alive during this time, offering the perfect opportunity to soak up the sunshine and savor the vibrant atmosphere.

2 Summer: Vibrant Festivities

Summer is when Leipzig truly comes alive with a plethora of festivals, events, and outdoor activities. From the legendary Wave-Gotik-Treffen, Europe's largest gothic and alternative music festival, to the

Leipzig Bach Festival, celebrating the city's most famous resident, there's no shortage of cultural experiences to enjoy. Outdoor enthusiasts can take advantage of the warm weather to explore Leipzig's scenic surroundings, whether it's cycling along the Elster Cycle Path or taking a boat tour along the picturesque River Elbe.

3 Autumn: Golden Hues and Cultural Delights

As summer fades into autumn, Leipzig takes on a golden hue, casting a magical spell over the city. The crisp air and vibrant foliage make it the perfect time for leisurely strolls through Leipzig's historic streets or scenic countryside. Autumn also brings with it a rich cultural calendar, with events such as the Leipzig Book Fair and the Leipzig Jazz Days attracting visitors from far and wide. After a day of exploration, cozy up in one of Leipzig's traditional pubs or beer halls and savor hearty German cuisine paired with locally brewed beer.

4 Winter: Magical Wonders and Festive Cheer

Winter transforms Leipzig into a winter wonderland straight out of a fairytale. The city's historic architecture is adorned with twinkling lights and festive decorations, creating a magical atmosphere that is sure to enchant visitors of all ages. Leipzig's Christmas markets are a highlight of the season, offering an array of traditional treats, handcrafted gifts, and seasonal delights. Don't miss the Leipzig Christmas Market, one of the oldest and largest in Germany, where the scent of mulled wine and roasted chestnuts fills the air, and carolers serenade passersby with festive tunes.

Any Time is the Right Time
There's never a wrong time to visit Leipzig. Whether you're drawn to the blossoming beauty of spring, the vibrant festivities of summer, the golden hues of autumn, or the magical wonders of winter, Leipzig offers a wealth of experiences throughout the year. So pack your bags and prepare to embark on an unforgettable journey through this captivating city, no matter the season.

Exploring Leipzig Transportation

Leipzig is a city full of dynamic energy and exciting discoveries. As you explore this metropolis, you'll find yourself eager to uncover its many treasures. Before embarking on your journey, let's dive into how to navigate Leipzig's transportation system with ease and confidence.

1. Public Transportation

Leipzig boasts an efficient and extensive public transportation network that makes getting around the city a breeze. Whether you're traveling by tram, bus, or S-Bahn (suburban railway), you'll find that Leipzig's public transport system is reliable, punctual, and easy to use.

Trams

Trams are the heart of Leipzig's public transportation system, weaving their way through the city streets and connecting you to key destinations. With over a dozen tram lines crisscrossing the city, you'll have no trouble reaching popular attractions, shopping districts, and cultural landmarks. Look out for the distinctive yellow and white trams as they glide gracefully through the streets, offering a scenic and convenient way to explore Leipzig.

Buses

In addition to trams, Leipzig's bus network provides another convenient option for getting around. Buses serve areas not covered by trams, making them ideal for reaching neighborhoods and sights off the beaten path. Whether you're heading to the Leipzig Zoo, the Monument to the Battle of the Nations, or simply navigating your way through the city, buses offer flexibility and accessibility.

S-Bahn

For journeys beyond the city center, Leipzig's S-Bahn system offers rapid transit connections to neighboring towns and suburbs. Whether you're planning a day trip to picturesque towns like Halle or Dresden, or simply need to travel to the outskirts of Leipzig, the S-Bahn provides a fast and efficient way to reach your destination.

2. Understanding Leipzig's Ticketing System

Now that you're familiar with Leipzig's modes of transportation, let's talk about how to pay for your journey. Leipzig's ticketing system is straightforward and user-friendly, designed to make your travel experience as smooth as possible.

Single Tickets
For occasional travelers, single tickets are the way to go. These tickets are valid for a single journey on either trams, buses, or the S-Bahn, allowing you to hop on and off as you please within a specified time frame.

Day Tickets
If you plan on exploring Leipzig extensively, consider purchasing a day ticket. Day tickets offer unlimited travel on all modes of public transportation within the city for an entire day, making them a cost-effective option for visitors and locals alike.

Leipzig Card
For travelers looking to combine transportation with sightseeing, the Leipzig Card is a fantastic choice. In addition to providing unlimited travel on Leipzig's public transport network, the Leipzig Card offers discounts on admission to museums, galleries, and other attractions, making it a great value for those wishing to take advantage of all that the city has to offer culturally.

3. Navigating Leipzig by Bicycle
For those who prefer a more active and eco-friendly mode of transportation, Leipzig is a cyclist's paradise. With its extensive network of bike lanes and flat terrain, Leipzig is perfect for exploring on

two wheels. Whether you're cruising along the picturesque paths of the Leipzig Riverside Forest or pedaling through the charming streets of the city center, cycling offers a unique perspective on Leipzig's beauty and charm.

Bike Rentals
Don't have your own bike? Not to worry! Leipzig offers numerous bike rental services, allowing you to easily rent a bike for a few hours or a full day. With options ranging from traditional bicycles to e-bikes, you'll find the perfect ride to suit your needs and preferences.

Bike-Friendly Infrastructure
Leipzig's commitment to cycling is evident in its bike-friendly infrastructure, which includes dedicated bike lanes, bike racks, and bike-friendly public transportation options. Whether you're commuting to work, running errands, or exploring the city, Leipzig makes it easy and safe to travel by bike.

4. Exploring Leipzig on Foot
Last but not least, don't underestimate the joy of exploring Leipzig on foot. With its compact size and pedestrian-friendly streets, Leipzig invites you to wander and discover its hidden gems at your own pace. From the historic streets of the Old Town to the bustling squares and parks, Leipzig's walkable

layout makes it the perfect city for leisurely strolls and spontaneous adventures.

Walking Tours
To enhance your experience of Leipzig on foot, consider joining a guided walking tour. Led by knowledgeable locals, these tours offer fascinating insights into Leipzig's history, architecture, and culture, allowing you to see the city through new eyes and connect with its rich heritage.

As you can see, getting around Leipzig is a breeze thanks to its efficient public transportation system, bike-friendly infrastructure, and walkable streets. Whether you're traveling solo, with friends, or with family, Leipzig offers a variety of transportation options to suit your needs and preferences. So go ahead, explore this enchanting city with confidence and curiosity, and let Leipzig's charm captivate you at every turn. Safe travels!

Essential Items for Leipzig

Packing for a trip can be a daunting task, especially when you're heading to a vibrant and multifaceted destination like Leipzig. Whether you're visiting for a few days or planning an extended stay, ensuring you have everything you need will make your journey more enjoyable and stress-free. This chapter will guide you through the essential items to pack for Leipzig, providing clear and encouraging advice to help you prepare effectively.

Clothing
Dressing for the Weather and Activities
Leipzig experiences a temperate seasonal climate, so your packing list should vary depending on the time of year.

Spring (March to May): Spring in Leipzig is mild, with temperatures ranging from 10°C to 20°C (50°F to 68°F). Pack light jackets, sweaters, and layers you can easily add or remove. A mix of long and short-sleeve shirts, as well as a pair of comfortable jeans or trousers, will serve you well. Don't forget a raincoat or a small umbrella, as spring showers are common.

Summer (June to August): Summers in Leipzig can be warm, with temperatures averaging between 20°C to 30°C (68°F to 86°F). Light, breathable clothing is essential. Think t-shirts, shorts, skirts, and sundressesTo effectively shield oneself from the sun, wear a hat and shades. However, also pack a light sweater or jacket for cooler evenings.

Autumn (September to November): Autumn brings cooler weather, with temperatures ranging from 10°C to 20°C (50°F to 68°F). Layering is key during this season. Pack sweaters, long-sleeve shirts, and light jackets. Comfortable walking shoes are a must, as you'll want to explore Leipzig's beautiful fall foliage.

Winter (December to February): Winters in Leipzig can be cold, with temperatures often below freezing, averaging between -1°C to 4°C (30°F to 39°F). Pack a heavy coat, scarves, gloves, and a warm hat. Layering with thermal underwear, sweaters, and long pants will keep you cozy. Waterproof boots are also essential to navigate any snow or slush.

Versatile and Comfortable Attire
Regardless of the season, it's important to pack versatile clothing that can be mixed and matched. This ensures you're prepared for various activities without overpacking.

Comfortable Shoes: Leipzig is a city best explored on foot. Pack a pair of comfortable walking shoes or sneakers for daytime exploration and another pair for evening outings. If you plan to attend any formal events or dine in upscale restaurants, consider bringing a pair of dress shoes.

Smart Casual Outfits: Leipzig boasts a lively cultural scene, including theaters, concerts, and art galleries. Pack a few smart-casual outfits that can be dressed up or down depending on the occasion. For instance, a nice pair of trousers or a skirt paired with a blouse or a button-down shirt can transition from day to night with ease.

Sportswear: If you enjoy outdoor activities, such as biking or hiking, include appropriate sportswear in your packing list. Athletic clothing, comfortable workout shoes, and a small backpack for day trips will come in handy.

Travel Essentials
Passport and Visa: Ensure your passport is valid for at least six months beyond your travel dates. Depending on your nationality, check if you need a visa to enter Germany and make arrangements accordingly.

Travel Insurance: Travel insurance is a safety net that covers unforeseen events, such as medical emergencies, trip cancellations, or lost luggage. Carry copies of your insurance policy and your emergency contact information at all times.

Money and Cards: Carry a combination of cash (euros) and credit/debit cards. While most places in Leipzig accept cards, having some cash is useful for small purchases or places that don't accept cards. Inform your bank of your travel dates to avoid any issues with card transactions.

Copies of Important Documents: Make photocopies or digital scans of important documents, such as your passport, visa, insurance, and itinerary. Store these copies separately from the originals and consider emailing them to yourself for easy access.

Electronics and Gadgets
Smartphone and Charger:A smartphone is indispensable for navigation, communication, and capturing memories. Ensure you have a compatible charger and, if necessary, an adapter for European outlets.

Power Bank: Keep your devices charged on the go with a power bank. This is particularly helpful on exhausting sightseeing days.

Camera: While smartphones have excellent cameras, you might want to bring a dedicated camera if you're passionate about photography. Keep in mind to bring spare batteries and memory cards.

Laptop or Tablet: If you plan to work or stay connected during your trip, a laptop or tablet can be useful. Ensure you have all necessary chargers and adapters.

Universal Adapter: Germany uses the Type C (two round pins) and Type F (two round pins with two earth clips) plugs. A universal adapter will ensure you can charge all your devices without hassle.

Personal Care and Health

Toiletries: Pack travel-sized toiletries to save space. Essential items include toothpaste, toothbrush, shampoo, conditioner, soap, deodorant, and any other personal hygiene products you use daily. Consider solid versions of these items to avoid liquid restrictions.

Medications: Bring any prescription medications you need, along with a copy of the prescription. Over-the-counter medications for common ailments, such as pain relievers, allergy meds, and stomach remedies, can also be useful.

First Aid Kit: A basic first aid kit with band-aids, antiseptic wipes, and other essentials can come in handy for minor injuries.

Skincare and Sun Protection: Include moisturizer, lip balm, and sunscreen in your packing list. The weather in Leipzig can vary, and it's important to protect your skin from both the sun and the cold.

Luggage and Organization
Suitcase or Backpack: Your choice of luggage depends on your travel style. A sturdy suitcase with wheels is ideal for those staying in one place, while a backpack might be better for those planning to move around frequently or travel on public transportation.

Carry-On Bag: A small carry-on bag or backpack is useful for keeping essentials within reach during your flight and for daily use while exploring the city. Choose a bag that's comfortable to carry and has enough space for your day-to-day items.

With thoughtful preparation and careful packing, you'll be well-equipped for your adventure in Leipzig. This captivating city, with its rich history, vibrant culture, and stunning architecture, awaits you. Enjoy your travels, and make the most of every moment in this beautiful German gem. Safe journey!

Entry and Visa Requirements for Leipzig

Traveling to Leipzig in Germany, known for its captivating blend of historical charm and modern attractions, requires careful preparation, especially regarding entry and visa requirements. Whether you are visiting for tourism, business, study, or to experience its renowned music festivals, understanding the visa and entry regulations is crucial to ensure a smooth and hassle-free journey. This chapter aims to provide comprehensive information on the necessary documentation, visa types, application processes, and other essential details to help travelers of all backgrounds navigate the entry requirements for Leipzig.

Leipzig is part of Germany, a member of the Schengen Area—a group of 27 European countries that have abolished internal borders, allowing free and unrestricted movement of people. Consequently, the entry requirements for Leipzig are governed by Schengen visa regulations.

Schengen Visa Basics

A Schengen visa allows travelers to move freely within the Schengen Zone for short stays up to 90 days within a 180-day period. This visa is suitable for tourism, family visits, short business trips, and other similar activities. There are various types of Schengen visas, each catering to different purposes and durations of stay.

Visa Exemptions

Citizens of several countries do not need a visa to enter Leipzig for short stays. These include EU/EEA member states, Switzerland, and many countries with visa waiver agreements with the Schengen Area, such as the United States, Canada, Australia, Japan, and South Korea. Travelers from these countries can stay in Leipzig and other Schengen countries for up to 90 days within any 180-day period without a visa.

ETIAS: An Upcoming Requirement

Starting from 2024, travelers from visa-exempt countries will need to apply for an ETIAS (European Travel Information and Authorization System) before their trip. ETIAS is a pre-travel authorization similar to the U.S. ESTA, aimed at enhancing security and managing travel more effectively. The application process is straightforward, involving an online form and a small fee.

Types of Visas

Travelers requiring a visa to enter Leipzig must apply for a Schengen visa. There are several types based on the purpose and duration of stay:

Short-Stay Visa (Type C)

The short-stay visa, or Type C visa, is the most common Schengen visa. It allows for stays up to 90 days within a 180-day period. This visa is suitable for:

Tourism: Exploring Leipzig's historical sites, cultural attractions, and festivals.
Business: Attending meetings, conferences, or exhibitions in Leipzig.
Family Visits: Visiting family or friends residing in Leipzig.
Short-term Studies or Training Participating in courses or training programs of less than three months.

Long-Stay Visa (Type D)

If you plan to stay in Leipzig for more than 90 days, you will need a long-stay visa or Type D visa. This visa is generally issued for purposes such as:

Employment: Working in Leipzig or other parts of Germany.
Study: Enrolling in a university or academic program.
Research: Conducting research at Leipzig's institutions.
Family Reunification: Joining family members who are residents or citizens of Germany.

Other Long-term Stays: For purposes not covered by the short-stay visa.

Airport Transit Visa (Type A)

An airport transit visa is required for travelers who need to transit through a German airport to reach their final destination outside the Schengen Area. This visa does not permit leaving the airport's international transit area.

Visa Application Process: Step-by-Step Guide
1. Determine the Type of Visa: Identify the appropriate visa type based on the purpose and duration of your stay.
2. Gather Required Documents: Collect all necessary documents, including:
1 appropriately completed and signed the visa application.
A valid passport with at least two blank pages and validity extending at least three months beyond your planned stay.
Passport-sized photos that satisfy the requirements for a Schengen visa
Proof of travel insurance covering medical emergencies with a minimum coverage of €30,000.
Proof of accommodation in Leipzig (hotel bookings, invitation letter, etc.).
Proof that you have the funds necessary to pay for your stay..
Detailed travel itinerary.

Supporting documents based on the purpose of the visit (e.g., invitation letter for business, admission letter for students).

3. Schedule an Appointment: Book an appointment at the nearest German embassy or consulate to submit your application and attend an interview if required.
4. Pay the Visa Fee: Pay the non-refundable visa application fee. The fee may vary based on the visa type and applicant's nationality.
5. Submit Your Application: Attend the appointment with all required documents. Biometrics (fingerprints and photograph) will be collected during the appointment.
6. Wait for Processing: Visa processing times can vary, typically ranging from 15 to 60 days.Applying well in advance of the dates you want to go is advised.
7. Receive Your Visa: Once approved, your visa will be affixed to your passport, allowing you to travel to Leipzig and the Schengen Area.

Different types of travelers may have unique considerations when applying for a visa to Leipzig.

1. Students
Students planning to study in Leipzig need to apply for a long-stay student visa (Type D). Essential documents include: An admission letter from a recognized Leipzig educational institution.
Verification that there is enough money for both living expenses and tuition.
Proof of accommodation.
Health insurance coverage.

Upon arrival, students must also register with the local authorities and obtain a residence permit for the duration of their studies.

2. Business Travelers
An invitation letter from the German company or organization detailing the purpose and duration of the visit. A letter from the applicant's employer stating the purpose of the visit and covering financial expenses.
Evidence of accommodation arrangements.

3. Tourists must present
Detailed travel itinerary, including accommodation and transport bookings. Proof of financial means for the duration of the stay.

Travel insurance policy meeting Schengen requirements.

Post-Arrival Requirements
After obtaining your visa and arriving in Leipzig, certain steps are essential to ensure compliance with local regulations.

Travelers staying longer than three months must register with the local residents' registration office (Einwohnermeldeamt) within 14 days of arrival. This registration is mandatory and involves providing proof of address and identification documents.

Residence Permit
Non-EU/EEA nationals staying for extended periods need to apply for a residence permit. This involves submitting additional documentation and may include proving financial stability, health insurance, and purpose of stay (employment, study, etc.).

Ensure you comply with the conditions of your visa, including the permitted duration of stay and purpose of visit. Overstaying or violating visa conditions can result in penalties, including fines, deportation, and future travel bans.

Understanding and adhering to the entry and visa requirements is crucial for a smooth and enjoyable visit to Leipzig. Whether you are visiting for a short stay or planning a longer-term move, thorough preparation and awareness of the necessary documentation and processes will help you navigate the journey with confidence. Remember to check the latest regulations and requirements from official sources or consult with the nearest German consulate or embassy to ensure all your documents are in order before embarking on your trip to this fascinating city.

Monetary Systems and Linguistics

The legacy and culture of Germany are greatly influenced by Leipzig, a thriving city in eastern Germany. Its economic and linguistic contexts have seen significant alteration over time. In order to demonstrate how language and currency have both affected and been influenced by Leipzig's evolution, this chapter examines the intricate link between the two factors. Our aim is to provide an in-depth understanding of Leipzig's unique blend of linguistic diversity and economic vigor through an analysis of both historical and contemporary conditions.

Leipzig's prominence as a trade hub dates back to the medieval period. Situated at the crossroads of major trade routes, it became a focal point for merchants from across Europe. During this era, the city's economy was bolstered by the Leipzig Trade Fair, one of the oldest of its kind, which attracted traders dealing in various currencies.

The currency used in Leipzig during the medieval period was predominantly the Mark, a common unit in the Holy Roman Empire. As trade expanded, foreign currencies such as the Italian florin and the Dutch guilder also circulated within the city. The presence of multiple currencies necessitated a robust understanding of exchange rates and financial transactions among the local populace, contributing to a rich economic culture.

Language played a crucial role in facilitating trade and commerce. German was the primary language spoken, but Latin served as the lingua franca for legal and scholarly purposes, particularly in contracts and correspondence. The influx of foreign merchants introduced other languages, including Italian, Dutch, and French, adding to the linguistic diversity. This multilingual environment fostered a culture of linguistic adaptability, crucial for successful trade negotiations.

The Industrial Revolution brought profound changes to Leipzig's economic landscape. The city emerged as a major center for publishing and the book trade, earning it the nickname "City of Books." The introduction of new technologies and industrial processes spurred economic growth and increased the demand for a standardized monetary system.

By the late 19th century, the German mark had become the dominant currency, reflecting the unification of Germany and the consolidation of its economic policies. The standardized currency facilitated smoother transactions and economic planning, which were essential for the burgeoning industrial sector.

The industrial boom also influenced linguistic practices in Leipzig. As the workforce expanded, so did the need for efficient communication. Standard German (Hochdeutsch) gained prominence in both business and education, gradually diminishing the regional dialects. Additionally, the influx of workers from different parts of Germany and beyond introduced new linguistic elements, enriching the local vernacular.

Leipzig's universities and research institutions attracted scholars from around the world, further enhancing its linguistic diversity. Academic discourse in Leipzig was often conducted in multiple languages, reflecting the city's status as an intellectual hub.

The 20th century was a period of significant economic upheaval for Leipzig. The World Wars, hyperinflation of the 1920s, and the division of Germany after World War II had profound impacts on the city's economy and currency. During the hyperinflation era, the value of the German mark plummeted, leading to the issuance of emergency currencies (Notgeld) by local authorities and businesses. These temporary currencies were often creatively designed and have since become collectors' items.

Following World War II, Leipzig found itself in the Soviet-occupied zone, eventually becoming part of the German Democratic Republic (GDR). The East German mark (Ostmark) became the official currency, and the centralized socialist economy dictated economic practices. The transition to a planned economy altered the financial landscape, with state-controlled pricing and limited private enterprise.

The political and economic changes of the 20th century also had linguistic repercussions. Under the GDR, Russian was emphasized as a second language due to the political alliance with the Soviet Union. This policy influenced education and professional communication, making Russian a significant part of the linguistic repertoire for many East Germans.

Despite the political pressure, German remained the primary language. However, the isolation from West Germany led to distinct linguistic developments. For instance, certain words and expressions unique to the GDR emerged, reflecting the different social and economic realities. The fall of the Berlin Wall in 1989 and the subsequent reunification of Germany in 1990 marked a new chapter for Leipzig. The transition from a socialist to a market economy brought both opportunities and challenges. The introduction of the Deutsche Mark (DM) in East Germany symbolized economic unification and a return to a capitalist economic framework. Leipzig underwent significant restructuring, with privatization and investment revitalizing its economy. The city attracted numerous businesses and industries, establishing itself as a major economic center in the newly unified Germany. The adoption of the euro in 2002 further integrated Leipzig into the broader European economy, facilitating international trade and investment.

Reunification also influenced linguistic practices in Leipzig. The reintegration with West Germany led to a homogenization of the German language, as media and cultural exchange flourished. Standard German became more prevalent, reducing regional linguistic variations.

English emerged as a crucial second language, driven by globalization and the need for international communication. Educational reforms emphasized English proficiency, preparing the younger generation for participation in the global economy. The presence of multinational companies and international institutions in Leipzig further reinforced the importance of English. Today, Leipzig stands as a dynamic economic hub within Germany. The city's economy is diversified, with key sectors including automotive manufacturing, information technology, and biotechnology. The presence of large corporations, such as BMW and Porsche, alongside a vibrant startup scene, underscores Leipzig's economic vitality. The euro, as the common currency of the European Union, facilitates seamless economic transactions within the region. The stability and strength of the euro contribute to Leipzig's attractiveness as a destination for investment and business. Additionally, the city's strategic location and well-developed infrastructure enhance its connectivity to other major European markets.

Leipzig's contemporary linguistic landscape is characterized by multilingualism and cultural exchange. German remains the predominant language, but the city's international outlook is reflected in the widespread use of English and other languages. The University of Leipzig, with its diverse student body, offers programs in multiple languages, fostering an inclusive academic environment.

Cultural events, such as the Leipzig Book Fair, attract visitors from around the world, further enriching the city's linguistic diversity. These events provide platforms for cultural exchange and highlight Leipzig's role as a cosmopolitan center. Additionally, initiatives promoting the learning of foreign languages contribute to the city's linguistic and cultural vibrancy. Leipzig's journey through history showcases the dynamic interplay between currency and language. From its medieval trading roots to its current status as an economic powerhouse, the city's economic fortunes and linguistic practices have been closely intertwined. The evolution of currency in Leipzig reflects broader economic transformations, while linguistic shifts mirror the city's adaptation to changing social and political landscapes.

Exploring Leipzig Affordably

For budget travelers, Leipzig, a city renowned for its dynamic cultural scene, youthful vitality, and rich history, has a wealth of things to offer. Leipzig is an excellent location for travelers who want to see new things without going over budget, thanks to its combination of historical sites, lovely parks, and reasonably priced food alternatives. This chapter will walk you through the elements of traveling to Leipzig on a budget, so you can maximize your time there while controlling your spending.

By Train
Leipzig is well-connected by rail, with frequent and affordable services from major cities in Germany and neighboring countries. Deutsche Bahn offers various discounts, such as the "Sparpreis" tickets, which can significantly reduce travel costs if booked early. Additionally, regional trains like the S-Bahn and RE (Regional Express) services are both efficient and economical, providing a scenic and relaxed way to travel.

By Bus
Long-distance buses are another budget-friendly option. Companies like FlixBus and Eurolines offer routes to Leipzig from numerous European cities at

low prices. While bus travel might take longer than trains, it's a great way to save money and often comes with amenities like free Wi-Fi and comfortable seating.

Budget Hotels and Guesthouses

If you prefer a bit more privacy, budget hotels and guesthouses are plentiful in Leipzig. Websites like Booking.com and Airbnb list numerous options that offer comfort without high costs. Look for places slightly outside the city center to find better deals, as public transport in Leipzig is efficient and affordable.

Couchsurfing

For the truly budget-conscious, Couchsurfing can be a fantastic way to save on accommodation while experiencing local hospitality. The Couchsurfing community in Leipzig is active, and staying with a local can provide unique insights into the city's culture and hidden gems.

Affordable Dining

Eating out in Leipzig doesn't have to be expensive. There are numerous eateries where you can enjoy traditional German cuisine at reasonable prices. Look for "Imbiss" stands and small local restaurants offering hearty dishes like bratwurst, schnitzel, and sauerkraut.

International Cuisine
Leipzig's culinary scene is diverse, with plenty of international options that won't strain your wallet. Consider trying out the city's numerous Turkish döner kebab shops, Vietnamese pho restaurants, and Italian pizzerias for delicious and affordable meals.

Markets and Street Food
Exploring local markets is both a culinary adventure and a budget-friendly option. The Leipzig Market Square hosts regular farmers' markets where you can buy fresh produce, local cheeses, and baked goods at reasonable prices. Additionally, street food festivals and pop-up markets are common, providing opportunities to sample diverse and affordable eats.

Free and Low-Cost Attractions
Leipzig is rich in history, and many of its landmarks can be enjoyed for free or at a low cost. Key historical sites include:

Parks and Gardens
Leipzig is home to numerous parks and green spaces that are perfect for relaxing and enjoying nature without spending a dime.

Shopping on a Budget
Leipzig offers a range of shopping experiences, from high-end boutiques to budget-friendly stores and markets.

Second-Hand Stores: Leipzig has many second-hand shops where you can find clothes, books, and household items at bargain prices. Some popular ones include Humana and Oxfam. Visiting Leipzig on a budget is entirely possible and immensely rewarding. By taking advantage of affordable accommodation, budget-friendly dining options, and the city's many free attractions, you can enjoy a rich and diverse travel experience without spending a fortune. With careful planning and a spirit of adventure, Leipzig's vibrant culture, historical depth, and welcoming atmosphere are yours to explore. So pack your bags, plan your itinerary, and get ready to discover the charms of Leipzig without breaking the bank.

Best Platforms to Book Your Leipzig Trip

Planning a trip to Leipzig? Choosing the right platforms to book your accommodations, transportation, and activities can make a significant difference in your travel experience. In this chapter, we'll explore some of the best places to book your Leipzig trip, ensuring convenience, affordability, and peace of mind throughout your journey.

Accommodations

Booking.com offers a vast selection of accommodations in Leipzig, ranging from budget-friendly hostels to luxury hotels and everything in between. The platform provides detailed information, user reviews, and flexible booking options, making it easy to find the perfect place to stay within your budget and preferences.

Airbnb

For travelers seeking a more personalized experience, Airbnb offers a wide range of apartments, houses, and unique properties in Leipzig. Whether you're looking for a cozy apartment in the city center or a charming guesthouse in a residential neighborhood, Airbnb allows you to connect directly with hosts and customize your stay according to your needs.

Activities and Tours
GetYourGuide is a popular platform for booking guided tours, activities, and experiences in Leipzig and beyond. Whether you're interested in historical walking tours, culinary adventures, or outdoor excursions, GetYourGuide offers a wide range of options curated by local experts. Booking through the platform provides peace of mind with secure payments, flexible cancellation policies, and 24/7 customer support.

Viator
Viator, a subsidiary of TripAdvisor, is another trusted platform for booking tours and activities worldwide. From sightseeing tours and museum passes to day trips and cultural experiences, Viator offers a diverse selection of activities tailored to every traveler's interests and preferences. With hassle-free booking and verified reviews from fellow travelers, Viator ensures a seamless booking process and memorable travel experiences.

Local Tourist Information Centers
For personalized recommendations and insider tips, consider visiting Leipzig's tourist information centers upon arrival. Located in prominent areas such as the Leipzig Hauptbahnhof (main train station) and the city center, these centers provide maps, brochures, and assistance from

knowledgeable staff members who can help you plan your itinerary, book tickets, and discover hidden gems off the beaten path.

Loyalty Programs and Discounts

Many travel booking platforms and transportation companies offer loyalty programs, discounts, and promotional codes for frequent travelers. By signing up for newsletters, creating accounts, or participating in loyalty programs, you can access exclusive deals, earn rewards points, and save money on future bookings.

Package Deals and Bundles

Consider booking package deals or bundled offers that include accommodations, transportation, and activities for added savings and convenience. Many travel agencies and online platforms offer discounted packages that combine multiple components of your trip into a single booking, allowing you to streamline the planning process and enjoy cost-effective travel experiences.

Flexible Booking Policies

When booking your Leipzig trip, prioritize platforms and providers with flexible booking policies, especially during uncertain times. Look for options that offer free cancellations, flexible rescheduling, and refundable deposits to accommodate changes in your travel plans or unexpected circumstances.

Choosing the right platforms to book your Leipzig trip can enhance your travel experience and ensure a seamless journey from start to finish. Whether you're searching for accommodations, transportation, activities, or local experiences, these trusted resources offer convenience, affordability, and peace of mind, allowing you to make the most of your time in this vibrant city.

CHAPTER 2
ICONIC ATTRACTIONS AND
LANDMARKS TO VISIT

St. Thomas Church (Thomaskirche)

Situated in the heart of Leipzig, St. Thomas Church (Thomaskirche) stands as a beacon of history, culture, and spirituality. This Gothic marvel, with its intricate architecture and storied past, is more than just a church—it is a symbol of Leipzig's rich cultural tapestry. From its association with Johann Sebastian Bach to its role in the city's historical events, St. Thomas Church is a must-see landmark that captivates visitors from around the world.

As you approach St. Thomas Church, the first thing that strikes you is its stunning Gothic architecture. The church's towering spires reach toward the sky, creating a majestic silhouette against the backdrop of Leipzig's skyline. The detailed stone carvings and the expansive stained-glass windows invite you to take a closer look. Each element of the church's exterior tells a story, from the intricately carved statues of saints to the soaring arches that symbolize the heavens.

Walking through the massive wooden doors of St. Thomas Church, you are greeted by a sense of awe. The high vaulted ceilings, supported by grand columns, draw your eyes upward, inspiring a feeling of reverence. The interior is filled with light filtering through the stained-glass windows, casting colorful patterns on the stone floor. It's easy to imagine the centuries of history and worship that have taken place within these walls.

St. Thomas Church is perhaps most famous for its connection to Johann Sebastian Bach, one of the greatest composers of all time. Bach served as the choir director at St. Thomas From 1723 until his passing in 1750, Thomas. His legacy is still very much alive in the church, making it a pilgrimage site for music lovers and Bach enthusiasts.

My first visit to St. Thomas Church was on a sunny afternoon. As I stepped inside, the cool air and the quiet ambiance immediately embraced me. I remember standing in the nave, taking in the grandeur of the space. The tranquility was palpable, and for a moment, I felt as if I had stepped back in time. The church also houses a Bach Museum, where I spent a good hour exploring. The exhibits include original manuscripts, Bach's personal belongings, and interactive displays that provide insight into his life and work. The museum does an excellent job of contextualizing Bach's contributions, making it accessible and engaging for visitors of all ages.

Beyond its musical heritage, St. Thomas Church has played a significant role in Leipzig's history. The church has witnessed numerous historical events and has been a center of community life for centuries. During the Reformation, it was a hub for the dissemination of Martin Luther's ideas. The church's embrace of Luther's teachings is evident in its architecture and artwork, which reflect the Protestant ethos.

One of the most poignant moments in the church's history occurred during the peaceful protests against the communist regime in East Germany. In the late 1980s, St. Thomas Church, along with St. Nicholas Church, became a gathering place for demonstrators advocating for freedom and human rights. These peaceful protests were instrumental in the eventual fall of the Berlin Wall, marking the church as a symbol of hope and resilience.

As you explore St. Thomas Church, take the time to appreciate the intricate details of its architecture. The nave is adorned with beautiful frescoes and carvings that depict biblical scenes and saints. The pulpit, with its elaborate design, is a masterpiece of craftsmanship. The church's organ, a central feature, is considered one of the finest in Europe. It's a treat to hear it played, especially during one of the regular concerts held at the church. The exterior of the church is equally impressive. The spire, which was added in the late 19th century, offers stunning views of Leipzig. Climbing to the top of the spire is an adventure in itself, but the panoramic view from the top is worth every step. From this vantage point, you can see the entire city, with its mix of historical and modern architecture, green spaces, and bustling streets.

St. Thomas Church is not just a historical monument; it is also a living, breathing part of the Leipzig community. Regular worship services, concerts, and community events keep the church vibrant and relevant. Visitors are welcome to attend services, where they can experience the church's spiritual atmosphere and join the congregation in worship.

Among my most treasured memories from St. Thomas Church was attending a Sunday service. The church was filled with locals and tourists alike, all coming together to share in the service. The choir's performance was breathtaking, and the sermon, though in German, conveyed a sense of unity and peace that transcends language barriers. After the service, the church courtyard buzzed with conversation as people gathered to socialize and reflect on the experience.

When planning your visit to St. Thomas Church, it's helpful to know a few practical details. The church is centrally located and easily accessible by public transportation. If you're driving, there are several parking options nearby. The church is open to visitors daily, but it's a good idea to check the schedule in advance, especially if you want to attend a service or concert. St. Thomas Church (Thomaskirche) is a treasure trove of history, culture, and spirituality. Its magnificent architecture, rich musical heritage, and significant role in historical events make it a landmark that should not be missed. Regardless of your interests—music lovers, history buffs, or just plain inquisitive tourists—St.Thomas Church offers something for everyone.

Leipzig Zoo (Zoologischer Garten Leipzig)

Leipzig Zoo, known locally as Zoologischer Garten Leipzig, stands as one of Germany's most celebrated and historically rich zoological parks. Established in 1878, it has evolved from a modest collection of animals into a world-renowned center for conservation, education, and recreation. This chapter delves into the unique aspects of Leipzig Zoo, highlighting its history, key attractions, conservation efforts, and personal experiences that illuminate its charm and significance.

Leipzig Zoo's origins can be traced back to the late 19th century when it was founded by Ernst Pinkert, a pioneering entrepreneur and animal enthusiast. Initially, the zoo featured a small assortment of native and exotic animals, catering to the curiosity of Leipzig's citizens and visitors. Over the decades, the zoo expanded both in size and in the diversity of its animal collection, reflecting the growing public interest in wildlife and conservation.

One of the pivotal moments in the zoo's history was the construction of the Aquarium and Terrarium House in the early 20th century, which introduced marine and reptilian life to its visitors. This period also saw the development of more naturalistic enclosures, moving away from the traditional barred cages to environments that more closely mimicked the animals' natural habitats.

Entering Gondwanaland, visitors are immediately transported to a lush, tropical environment that feels worlds away from the city of Leipzig. This vast indoor rainforest, spanning 1.65 hectares, is home to over 100 exotic animal species and 500 plant species from the continents of Africa, Asia, and South America. The humid air, the sound of cascading waterfalls, and the sight of free-flying birds create an immersive experience that captivates all senses.

One of my most memorable experiences in Gondwanaland was the boat ride along the artificial river, which offered a unique perspective of the diverse flora and fauna. Gliding past the enclosures, I saw pygmy hippos lounging in the water, spider monkeys swinging from tree branches, and colorful tropical birds perched high above. The knowledgeable guides provided fascinating insights into the ecosystems represented in Gondwanaland and the conservation efforts undertaken to protect them. Pongoland is another highlight of Leipzig Zoo, dedicated to the study and conservation of our closest animal relatives: the great apes. This area is not just an exhibit but a research center in collaboration with the Max Planck Institute for Evolutionary Anthropology. It provides valuable data on the behavior, communication, and social structures of chimpanzees, bonobos, gorillas, and orangutans. Walking through Pongoland, visitors can observe these magnificent creatures in spacious and enriching environments designed to stimulate their natural behaviors. One poignant moment for me was watching a group of gorillas interact, displaying a range of emotions and social bonds that are strikingly similar to humans. Informative displays and interactive elements further enhance the educational aspect of the visit, making it both engaging and enlightening.

Leipzig Zoo is not only a place for public enjoyment but also a vital center for conservation and research. The zoo actively participates in numerous international breeding programs for endangered species, contributing to the preservation of biodiversity. Species such as the Amur leopard, Sumatran tiger, and various primates are part of these critical efforts.

One of the zoo's flagship conservation projects is the EAZA (European Association of Zoos and Aquaria) ex situ breeding program, which aims to create genetically diverse populations of endangered species in captivity. These efforts are complemented by in situ conservation initiatives, where the zoo collaborates with global partners to protect natural habitats and support local communities in regions where these species are native. The zoo's commitment to research is exemplified by its partnerships with academic institutions. Studies on animal behavior, genetics, and veterinary medicine conducted at Leipzig Zoo have yielded valuable insights that inform both in-zoo care and wild conservation strategies. Pongoland, in particular, has been a hub for groundbreaking research on primate cognition and social behavior.

Education is a cornerstone of Leipzig Zoo's mission. The zoo offers a range of programs designed to inspire and inform visitors of all ages about wildlife and conservation. From guided tours and interactive exhibits to workshops and school programs, there are ample opportunities for learning and engagement.

During my visit, I attended a fascinating presentation on the zoo's conservation efforts, which highlighted the interconnectedness of global ecosystems and the importance of protecting them. The use of multimedia, live demonstrations, and engaging storytelling made the session both informative and memorable. The zoo also hosts special events and themed days that celebrate biodiversity and raise awareness about specific conservation issues.

My visit to Leipzig Zoo was filled with moments of wonder and discovery. One particularly striking memory was witnessing the daily feeding of the penguins in the Polarium. The keepers shared fascinating facts about these charismatic birds, and seeing their agile movements both on land and underwater was a delight.

The zoo's vision for the future also includes fostering greater community involvement. Initiatives like volunteer programs, citizen science projects, and partnerships with local schools and organizations aim to engage the public in meaningful ways, fostering a sense of stewardship for the natural world.

Leipzig Zoo (Zoologischer Garten Leipzig) is more than just a place to see animals; it is a living testament to the power of conservation, education, and community engagement. From its historical roots to its modern-day achievements, the zoo embodies a commitment to preserving biodiversity and inspiring a love for wildlife. Whether you're exploring the tropical wonders of Gondwanaland, marveling at the great apes in Pongoland, or simply enjoying a leisurely stroll through its beautiful grounds, Leipzig Zoo offers an enlightening and remarkable encounter for guests of all ages.

Monument to the Battle of the Nations (Völkerschlachtdenkmal)

Standing majestically in Leipzig, Germany, the Monument to the Battle of the Nations (Völkerschlachtdenkmal) is a striking symbol of European history. Commemorating the Battle of Leipzig of 1813, this monument not only honors a pivotal military conflict but also serves as a testament to the unity and resilience of nations. We are about elves into the rich history, architectural grandeur, and enduring significance of the Völkerschlachtdenkmal, presenting an accessible narrative for readers of all backgrounds.

The idea to commemorate the Battle of Leipzig with a monument emerged in the 19th century, driven by a desire to celebrate national unity and military valor. However, it wasn't until the centennial of the battle in 1913 that the Völkerschlachtdenkmal was completed. The project was spearheaded by the German architect Bruno Schmitz, known for his grandiose designs. Schmitz's vision was ambitious. He designed a monument that would not only memorialize the battle but also stand as a landmark of architectural achievement. The foundation stone was laid in 1898, and over the next fifteen years, the monument rose, funded by public donations and supported by various patriotic organizations. The Völkerschlachtdenkmal was inaugurated on October 18, 1913, in a ceremony attended by numerous dignitaries, including Kaiser Wilhelm II. The exterior of the monument is dominated by a series of imposing statues and intricate reliefs. At the base, four colossal warrior figures guard the entrance, symbolizing the readiness to defend the homeland. These figures are flanked by smaller statues representing virtues such as bravery, faith, and sacrifice, underscoring the moral themes associated with the battle.

Upon entering, visitors are greeted by the grand central hall, a vast space designed to evoke awe. The hall's walls are adorned with reliefs depicting scenes from the battle, illustrating the chaos and heroism of the conflict. Above, a large dome allows light to filter in, illuminating the space in a way that enhances the monument's solemn atmosphere.

Beneath the central hall lies the crypt, a somber area containing statues of fallen warriors. These statues are designed to evoke a sense of mourning and remembrance, honoring the lives lost in the battle. The crypt's dim lighting and heavy stone architecture contribute to its reflective ambiance, inviting visitors to contemplate the sacrifices made during the conflict.

One of the monument's most popular features is the observation platform at the top. Visitors can ascend via a series of staircases and elevators, culminating in a panoramic view of Leipzig and its surroundings. This vantage point not only provides a breathtaking vista but also offers a symbolic perspective on the unity and resilience that the monument represents.

The Völkerschlachtdenkmal is rich with symbolism, reflecting themes of unity, sacrifice, and victory. Each element of its design is imbued with meaning, intended to convey the monument's historical and cultural significance.

The monument stands as a testament to the power of collective action. The coalition of nations that defeated Napoleon at Leipzig is commemorated through the diverse artistic elements that represent different European cultures. This unity in diversity is a central theme, symbolizing the strength that comes from collaboration.

Today, the Völkerschlachtdenkmal remains a major cultural and historical site. It attracts visitors from around the world, drawn by its architectural grandeur and historical significance. The monument has also become a venue for various cultural events, lectures, and commemorations, further cementing its role as a focal point of public memory.

Over the years, efforts have been made to preserve the Völkerschlachtdenkmal. Restoration projects have ensured that the monument remains in excellent condition, allowing future generations to appreciate its historical and cultural value. These efforts reflect a broader commitment to preserving historical sites as part of our shared heritage. The Monument to the Battle of the Nations (Völkerschlachtdenkmal) in Leipzig stands as a monumental tribute to one of Europe's most significant battles. Through its grand architecture, rich symbolism, and enduring significance, it tells the story of a pivotal moment in history.

St. Nicholas Church (Nikolaikirche)

St. Nicholas Church, known as Nikolaikirche in German, is one of Leipzig's most historic and culturally significant landmarks. This chapter explores the rich history, architectural beauty, and profound historical impact of Nikolaikirche, particularly its pivotal role in the Peaceful Revolution of 1989. With a narrative designed to be informative and accessible, this chapter aims to captivate readers and highlight the enduring importance of this remarkable church.

Nikolaikirche's architecture is a blend of various styles, resulting from the multiple phases of construction and renovation it has undergone. Each element of its design tells a story, contributing to the church's overall grandeur and historical significance.

The exterior of Nikolaikirche is characterized by its impressive Gothic spires and intricate stonework. The main entrance features ornate carvings and statues, typical of Gothic architecture, which convey religious themes and biblical scenes. The towering spires, added during the 15th century, dominate the Leipzig skyline and serve as a beacon for the city's faithful.

The interior of Nikolaikirche is equally impressive, with a stunning blend of Gothic and Baroque elements. The nave, with its high vaulted ceilings and elegant columns, creates a sense of spaciousness and grandeur. The church's Baroque altar, added in the 18th century, is a masterpiece of religious art, adorned with intricate sculptures and gold leaf.

Nikolaikirche is renowned for its musical heritage, particularly its association with Johann Sebastian Bach. Bach served as the Director of Music for Leipzig and frequently performed at Nikolaikirche. The church's organ, originally built in the 18th century and restored several times since, is one of its most treasured features. It continues to be used for concerts and services, maintaining the church's rich musical tradition.

The church's involvement in the revolution began with the "Monday Prayers for Peace," initiated by Pastor Christian Führer in 1982. These prayer meetings, held every Monday evening, provided a space for citizens to gather and express their desire for political change and human rights. Over time, the gatherings grew in size and significance, attracting thousands of participants.

Today, St. Nicholas Church continues to be a vital part of Leipzig's cultural and religious life. It serves as an active place of worship, a tourist attraction, and a venue for cultural events, reflecting its multifaceted significance. Nikolaikirche is also a venue for concerts, lectures, and other cultural events. Its exceptional acoustics and historic organ make it a popular location for classical music performances, particularly those celebrating the works of Johann Sebastian Bach. St. Nicholas Church (Nikolaikirche) in Leipzig is more than just a historic building; it is a living monument to the city's rich cultural and religious heritage.

Leipzig Hauptbahnhof

Leipzig Hauptbahnhof, or Leipzig Central Station, is not just a major transportation hub; it is an architectural marvel and a historical landmark. As one of the largest railway stations in Europe, Leipzig Hauptbahnhof plays a crucial role in the daily lives of millions of travelers and stands as a testament to the city's rich history and dynamic present.

Leipzig Hauptbahnhof is renowned for its impressive architecture, which combines functional design with aesthetic grandeur. Spanning a vast area of approximately 83,640 square meters, the station features a blend of classical and modern elements, making it both a practical facility and an architectural landmark.

Leipzig Hauptbahnhof is characterized by its monumental facade, which stretches over 300 meters in length. The facade is adorned with neoclassical elements, including columns, pilasters, and ornate stone carvings. These features convey a sense of grandeur and stability, befitting a major transportation hub. One of the most striking aspects of the exterior is the series of large arched windows, which allow natural light to flood the interior concourses. The main entrance is marked by an imposing portico, supported by Corinthian columns, leading into the vast interior spaces of the station. The interior of Leipzig Hauptbahnhof is equally impressive, with expansive halls and concourses designed to handle large volumes of passengers efficiently. The main concourse, known as the "Querbahnsteighalle," is a vast open space that connects the various platforms and services within the station. The high ceilings and large windows create a bright and airy environment, enhancing the overall passenger experience. One of the notable features of the interior is the intricate ironwork used in the construction of the platform canopies and other structural elements. This ironwork, combined with the use of glass and stone, gives the station a distinctive and elegant appearance.

Leipzig Hauptbahnhof has 26 platforms, making it one of the largest railway stations in Europe. The platforms are arranged in a U-shape, with most of the long-distance trains departing from the central platforms and regional and suburban trains using the outer platforms. This layout facilitates efficient passenger movement and minimizes congestion during peak travel times.

The station also features an extensive underground concourse, which provides access to additional platforms, shopping areas, and other amenities. This underground section is seamlessly integrated with the rest of the station, ensuring easy navigation for travelers.

Today, Leipzig Hauptbahnhof is a modern, well-equipped transportation hub that seamlessly blends its historical architecture with contemporary amenities. The station has undergone several phases of modernization to enhance its functionality and passenger experience. One of the standout features of Leipzig Hauptbahnhof is the extensive range of shopping and dining options available within the station. The Promenaden, a three-level shopping mall located within the station, offers a wide variety of retail stores, restaurants, and cafes. This integration of commercial services makes the station a destination in its own right, attracting both travelers and local residents.

Leipzig Hauptbahnhof is a crucial node in Germany's railway network, providing connections to numerous domestic and international destinations. The station is served by high-speed Intercity-Express (ICE) trains, regional trains, and local S-Bahn services, ensuring efficient and convenient travel options for passengers. The station also plays a role in community engagement and social initiatives. Various programs and events are organized to support local communities and promote social cohesion. This includes charity events, educational programs, and initiatives aimed at improving the overall passenger experience. Leipzig Hauptbahnhof stands as a testament to the city's rich history, architectural beauty, and dynamic present. From its origins in the 19th century to its role in major historical events and its modern-day significance, the station is a symbol of Leipzig's enduring importance as a transportation and cultural hub.

The Gewandhaus Orchestra

The Gewandhaus Orchestra, based in Leipzig, Germany, is one of the world's oldest and most renowned symphony orchestras. With a history dating back over 275 years, the orchestra's journey is a testament to the enduring power of music and its ability to transcend time, culture, and geography.

The Gewandhaus Orchestra's story begins in 1743 when a group of Leipzig's wealthy merchants and music enthusiasts founded a private concert society called the "Grosses Concert." These early concerts took place in private homes and small venues, but their popularity quickly grew. By 1781, the society had moved to a larger venue, the Gewandhaus, a building originally constructed as a trading hall for cloth merchants. This new home provided the orchestra with a stable base and marked the beginning of its formal existence as the Gewandhaus Orchestra. One of the most transformative periods in the Gewandhaus Orchestra's history came with the appointment of Felix Mendelssohn as its conductor in 1835. Mendelssohn, a prodigious composer and conductor, brought a new level of professionalism and artistic excellence to the orchestra. Under his leadership, the Gewandhaus Orchestra gained an international reputation, attracting audiences from across Europe.

Mendelssohn's influence extended beyond the concert hall. He was instrumental in establishing the Leipzig Conservatory, which became one of the most important music schools in Europe. Many of the Gewandhaus Orchestra's musicians were also teachers at the conservatory, creating a symbiotic relationship between education and performance that enriched the musical culture of Leipzig.

Throughout the 19th century, the Gewandhaus Orchestra continued to innovate and expand its repertoire. The orchestra was known for its adventurous programming, often premiering new works by contemporary composers. This spirit of innovation helped to keep the orchestra at the forefront of musical development, attracting composers such as Richard Wagner, who conducted the orchestra himself on several occasions.

The Gewandhaus Orchestra also played a crucial role in the popularization of large-scale symphonic works. Its performances of Beethoven's symphonies, in particular, were highly influential, helping to establish these works as central pillars of the orchestral repertoire. The orchestra's commitment to excellence and innovation set a standard that inspired other orchestras around the world.

In 1981, the orchestra celebrated the opening of a new concert hall, the third Gewandhaus, located in the heart of Leipzig. This state-of-the-art facility provided the orchestra with a modern home that matched its prestigious status. The new Gewandhaus was designed with acoustics in mind, ensuring that every performance could be heard with exceptional clarity and richness. The opening of the new hall was a symbolic moment, representing the orchestra's rebirth and its continued dedication to musical excellence.

Today, the Gewandhaus Orchestra remains one of the leading symphony orchestras in the world. Its musicians are drawn from a diverse pool of international talent, and its repertoire spans from the classical masterpieces of the past to cutting-edge contemporary works. The orchestra continues to uphold its tradition of innovation and excellence, commissioning new works and collaborating with some of the most exciting composers and conductors of our time.

One of the unique aspects of the Gewandhaus Orchestra is its commitment to community engagement. The orchestra offers a wide range of educational programs, from school concerts and workshops to masterclasses and outreach initiatives. These programs aim to inspire the next generation of musicians and music lovers, ensuring that the orchestra's rich legacy continues to thrive. The Gewandhaus Orchestra has been led by a remarkable lineage of conductors, each of whom has left an indelible mark on its history. From Mendelssohn to Kurt Masur, who served as the orchestra's music director from 1970 to 1996, these conductors have shaped the orchestra's sound and direction. Masur, in particular, is remembered for his passionate commitment to music and his role in fostering the orchestra's international reputation during the Cold War era.

The current music director, Andris Nelsons, continues this tradition of excellence. Nelsons, known for his dynamic and expressive conducting style, has brought new energy to the orchestra. Under his leadership, the Gewandhaus Orchestra has embarked on ambitious recording projects and international tours, further cementing its status as a global cultural ambassador.

Collaboration has always been at the heart of the Gewandhaus Orchestra's philosophy. The orchestra regularly works with leading soloists and ensembles, creating performances that are rich in diversity and artistic synergy. These collaborations allow the orchestra to explore a wide range of musical styles and genres, from classical to contemporary, from opera to jazz. Attending a concert at the Gewandhaus is more than just a musical performance; it is an experience that engages all the senses. The concert hall itself, with its stunning architecture and world-class acoustics, creates an atmosphere of grandeur and intimacy. The audience is treated to performances that are not only technically impeccable but also emotionally powerful, reflecting the deep connection between the musicians and the music they perform.

The Gewandhaus Orchestra is more than just a musical ensemble; it is a living legacy that embodies the rich history and vibrant culture of Leipzig. Its journey, marked by triumphs and challenges, reflects the universal power of music to uplift, inspire, and unite. As we celebrate the achievements of the past and look forward to the possibilities of the future, the Gewandhaus Orchestra stands as a shining example of what can be achieved through dedication, creativity, and a shared love of music. Whether you are a lifelong classical music enthusiast or a newcomer to the world of orchestral music, the Gewandhaus Orchestra offers an experience that is both timeless and transformative.

Leipzig Botanical Garden

Located within the bustling city of Leipzig lies a serene oasis of greenery and biodiversity: the Leipzig Botanical Garden. This chapter explores the rich history, diverse collections, and educational mission of this botanical treasure. From its humble beginnings to its current role as a center for conservation and research, the Leipzig Botanical Garden offers visitors a glimpse into the wonders of the natural world.

Today, the Leipzig Botanical Garden is home to an impressive array of plant collections, ranging from native flora to rare and endangered species from every corner of the globe. The garden's outdoor beds and greenhouses showcase a diverse array of plants, organized by geographic region, ecological habitat, and botanical classification.

One of the garden's most notable collections is its extensive assortment of orchids, which includes over 2,000 species and hybrids. These delicate and exotic flowers are housed in specialized greenhouses, where visitors can marvel at their beauty and diversity. In addition to orchids, the garden boasts collections of tropical rainforest plants, alpine flora, succulents, and carnivorous plants. Each collection is carefully curated and maintained by a team of dedicated botanists and horticulturists, ensuring that the plants thrive in their respective environments. Beyond its role as a public garden, the Leipzig Botanical Garden plays a vital role in conservation and research efforts. The garden is actively involved in the preservation of rare and endangered plant species, both through in-situ conservation projects and ex-situ collections.

Through partnerships with botanical institutions and conservation organizations around the world, the Leipzig Botanical Garden participates in seed banking, plant propagation, and habitat restoration initiatives. These efforts help to safeguard plant biodiversity and promote sustainable stewardship of natural resources.

The Leipzig Botanical Garden is committed to sharing its knowledge and passion for plants with the public. Through a variety of educational programs and outreach initiatives, the garden engages visitors of all ages in the wonders of the natural world.

Guided tours, workshops, and lectures provide opportunities for visitors to learn about plant biology, gardening techniques, and conservation practices. Special events, such as plant sales, festivals, and art exhibitions, offer unique experiences that inspire curiosity and appreciation for plants. The garden also serves as a living laboratory for amateur gardeners and plant enthusiasts, who come to seek inspiration and advice from its expert staff. Whether you're a seasoned gardener or just starting out, the Leipzig Botanical Garden offers a wealth of resources and expertise to help you cultivate your green thumb.

As we conclude our exploration of the Leipzig Botanical Garden, we are reminded of the profound impact that plants have on our lives and our planet. From the air we breathe to the food we eat, plants sustain us in countless ways, enriching our lives with their beauty, diversity, and resilience. Whether you're strolling through its lush gardens, marveling at its exotic blooms, or participating in a hands-on workshop, the Leipzig Botanical Garden invites you to embark on a journey of discovery and wonder. As you explore its pathways and pathways, may you find joy, inspiration, and a renewed connection to the incredible world of plants.

CHAPTER 3
EXPLORING LODGING CHOICES

Types of Accommodations Available

Leipzig, a vibrant metropolis brimming with cultural treasures, offers a wide array of accommodations to suit every traveler's needs. From luxurious hotels to budget-friendly hostels, the city has something for everyone. In this chapter, we will explore the various types of accommodations available in Leipzig, providing you with insights into what each type has to offer.

Hotels
Hotels are one of the most popular types of accommodation in Leipzig, ranging from high-end luxury establishments to more modest budget options. Luxury hotels in Leipzig, such as the Hotel Fürstenhof and Steigenberger Grandhotel Handelshof, provide top-tier services, including gourmet dining, spas, and elegantly furnished rooms. These hotels are perfect for those looking to indulge in comfort and sophistication. Mid-range hotels like Pentahotel Leipzig and Radisson Blu Hotel offer a balance of quality and affordability. They provide modern amenities, including fitness centers and on-site restaurants, ensuring a

comfortable stay without breaking the bank. For budget-conscious travelers, options like Ibis Budget Leipzig City and Motel One Leipzig-Augustusplatz offer clean, comfortable rooms at affordable rates. These hotels focus on providing essential amenities and a convenient location without unnecessary frills.

Apartments and Vacation Rentals
Apartments and vacation rentals are ideal for travelers seeking more space and the comforts of home. Serviced apartments such as those offered by Adina Apartment Hotel Leipzig and Capri by Fraser Leipzig provide fully furnished units with kitchens and living areas, along with hotel-like services including housekeeping and fitness centers. These accommodations are perfect for longer stays or families needing extra room.

Vacation rentals, available through platforms like Airbnb and Vrbo, offer a variety of options, from cozy studios to spacious family homes. Examples include Charming City Apartments, which provide modern decor and convenient locations, and larger properties like Spacious Family Home, ideal for groups and families. These rentals allow for a personalized and flexible lodging experience.

Guesthouses and Bed & Breakfasts
For a more intimate and personalized experience, guesthouses and bed & breakfasts (B&Bs) offer a

welcoming atmosphere. Guesthouses such as Pension Leipzig Georgplatz and Pension am Stadtrand provide comfortable rooms, often with breakfast included, and a homely feel. These accommodations are usually family-run, adding a personal touch to your stay.

B&Bs like Gästehaus Leipzig and B&B Blumenau Leipzig offer charming rooms with unique decor and homemade breakfasts. These lodgings emphasize hospitality and often feature historic or distinctive architecture, providing a memorable experience for guests.

Unique and Alternative Accommodations
Leipzig also boasts a variety of unique and alternative accommodations for those looking for something different. Boutique hotels such as INNSiDE by Meliá Leipzig and Hotel Fregehaus offer stylish and distinctive environments with personalized services. These hotels often feature creative designs and luxurious amenities, ensuring a unique stay.

Eco-friendly accommodations cater to environmentally conscious travelers. Options like Bio-Hotel Leipzig and Green Residence Leipzig prioritize sustainability through practices like using organic products and energy-efficient systems, allowing guests to enjoy their stay with a minimal ecological footprint.

Historic accommodations, such as Schloss Breitenfeld Hotel & Tagung and Hotel Michaelis, provide a glimpse into Leipzig's past. These lodgings, often set in beautifully restored buildings, combine historical charm with modern comforts, offering a unique and enriching experience.

Student Accommodations
Given Leipzig's status as a major educational center, the city offers various student accommodations that are affordable and conveniently located. University dormitories provided by Studentenwerk Leipzig offer basic, cost-effective lodging options close to university campuses. These dormitories typically include shared facilities and common areas, fostering a communal living experience.

Private student housing, such as BaseCamp Leipzig and The Fizz Leipzig, provides more amenities and flexibility compared to university dormitories. These residences offer furnished rooms, study areas, and social spaces, creating a vibrant and supportive environment for students. With its diverse range of accommodations, Leipzig ensures that every traveler can find a suitable place to stay. Whether you seek the luxury of a high-end hotel, the budget-friendly environment of a hostel, the comfort of an apartment, the personalized touch of a guesthouse, or the unique experience of a boutique or historic hotel, Leipzig has it all. This variety makes it easy to find accommodations that match your preferences and needs, ensuring a memorable and enjoyable stay in this captivating city.

Best Hotels and Resorts Leipzig

Leipzig, offers a delightful array of accommodations that cater to a variety of tastes and preferences. From luxurious five-star hotels to charming boutique establishments, Leipzig's hospitality scene reflects the city's unique blend of old-world elegance and modern vibrancy. In this chapter, we will explore some of the top hotels and resorts in Leipzig, highlighting their distinctive features, exceptional services, and how they contribute to an unforgettable stay in this fascinating city.

Hotel Fürstenhof Leipzig

Situated in a historic 18th-century building, Hotel Fürstenhof is one of Leipzig's most prestigious hotels. Its central location near the main train station and the historic city center makes it an ideal base for exploring the city's attractions. The hotel features elegantly furnished rooms and suites, each adorned with luxurious fabrics and classic decor. Guests can enjoy gourmet dining at the hotel's restaurant, Villers, which offers a refined menu of regional and international cuisine. The AquaMarin Spa provides a serene retreat with an indoor pool, sauna, and a range of therapeutic treatments.

Steigenberger Grandhotel Handelshof

Located in the heart of Leipzig, the Steigenberger Grandhotel Handelshof combines historical grandeur with contemporary luxury. The hotel is housed in a beautifully restored building that was once a trading house. Its rooms and suites are spacious and stylishly decorated, offering modern amenities and stunning views of the city. The Brasserie Le Grand offers a sophisticated dining experience with a focus on French cuisine, while the Spa World Premium provides a sanctuary for relaxation with its saunas, fitness center, and massage treatments. The hotel's prime location means that guests are just steps away from key landmarks such as the Leipzig Opera and St. Nicholas Church.

Hotel The Westin Leipzig

The Westin Leipzig is known for its sleek design and modern comforts. Located near the Leipzig Zoo and the main train station, this hotel offers convenient access to the city's major attractions. The Westin features elegantly appointed rooms and suites, many with panoramic views of Leipzig's skyline. Dining options include the Michelin-starred Falco Restaurant, which offers innovative cuisine in a stylish setting. The hotel's wellness area includes a large indoor pool, a sauna, and a well-equipped fitness center, ensuring guests can relax and rejuvenate during their stay.

Hotel Fregehaus

Situated in a beautifully restored 16th-century building, Hotel Fregehaus is a boutique hotel that exudes charm and character. Located in the city center, it offers easy access to Leipzig's vibrant cultural scene. Each of the hotel's rooms is individually decorated, combining antique furnishings with modern comforts. The hotel's courtyard is a tranquil oasis where guests can unwind after a day of exploring. Breakfast is served in a cozy lounge, featuring a selection of locally sourced organic products. Hotel Fregehaus is particularly known for its warm hospitality and personalized service, making it a favorite among travelers who seek a homely atmosphere.

Hotel Michaelis

Located in the historic Südvorstadt district, Hotel Michaelis is a charming boutique hotel housed in a late 19th-century building. The hotel offers a mix of traditional elegance and modern convenience, with rooms that feature classic decor and contemporary amenities. The in-house restaurant, Michaelis, is renowned for its gourmet cuisine, emphasizing regional and seasonal ingredients. The hotel also has beautiful gardens where guests can relax in a serene environment. Hotel Michaelis is known for its friendly service and attention to detail, providing a welcoming retreat for visitors to Leipzig.

Gästehaus Leipzig

Gästehaus Leipzig offers a cozy and affordable option for travelers who prefer a homely atmosphere. Located near the city center, this guesthouse provides easy access to many of Leipzig's attractions. The rooms are comfortably furnished and come with modern amenities, ensuring a pleasant stay. A continental breakfast is served daily, and guests can enjoy complimentary coffee and tea throughout the day. The friendly staff are always available to provide recommendations and assist with travel arrangements. Gästehaus Leipzig is perfect for those who want a comfortable and welcoming place to stay without breaking the bank.

Leipzig offers a diverse range of accommodations that cater to every traveler's needs, from luxurious five-star hotels to charming boutique establishments and eco-friendly options. Each of these hotels and resorts provides a unique experience, whether you are looking for historical charm, modern luxury, personalized service, or sustainability. By choosing to stay at one of these top hotels and resorts in Leipzig, you can ensure that your visit to this captivating city is as comfortable and memorable as possible

Budget-Friendly Options

Traveling on a budget doesn't mean sacrificing comfort or missing out on a rich experience, especially in a vibrant city like Leipzig. With its wide range of affordable accommodations, from cozy hostels to budget-friendly hotels and guesthouses, Leipzig caters to travelers looking to make the most of their visit without breaking the bank. In this chapter, we will explore some of the best budget-friendly options in Leipzig, offering insights into their amenities, locations, and unique features that make them ideal for cost-conscious travelers.

Ibis Budget Leipzig City

Located in the heart of Leipzig, Ibis Budget Leipzig City offers a perfect blend of affordability and convenience. This hotel is just a short walk from the main train station and many of Leipzig's top attractions, including the Leipzig Opera and St. Nicholas Church. The rooms are compact but well-designed, featuring comfortable beds, free Wi-Fi, and modern amenities. The hotel offers a daily breakfast buffet at an additional cost, providing a variety of options to start your day. With its central location and reliable service, Ibis Budget Leipzig City is an excellent choice for budget travelers.

B&B Hotel Leipzig-City

Another great option in the city center, B&B Hotel Leipzig-City provides modern accommodations at an affordable price. This hotel is known for its clean and comfortable rooms, each equipped with air conditioning, free Wi-Fi, and flat-screen TVs. The hotel offers a breakfast buffet with a wide selection of items to suit different tastes. Its central location makes it easy to explore Leipzig's attractions, such as the Leipzig Zoo and the Museum of Fine Arts. The B&B Hotel Leipzig-City is ideal for travelers who want a comfortable and budget-friendly place to stay while enjoying the city.

Motel One Leipzig-Augustusplatz

Motel One is a well-known budget hotel chain that combines stylish design with affordability. The Leipzig-Augustusplatz location is no exception, offering chic and comfortable rooms in the heart of the city. Each room is designed with modern decor, featuring high-quality beds, free Wi-Fi, and flat-screen TVs. The hotel's One Lounge serves as a breakfast area, bar, and café, providing a relaxed atmosphere for guests. Its prime location near Augustusplatz means that many of Leipzig's landmarks and cultural sites are within walking distance. Motel One Leipzig-Augustusplatz is perfect for travelers who appreciate style and comfort on a budget.

Sleepy Lion Hostel, Youth Hotel & Apartments Leipzig

Located just a short walk from the city center, Sleepy Lion Hostel is a popular choice for budget-conscious travelers. The hostel offers a variety of accommodation options, including private rooms, dormitories, and apartments, catering to different preferences and budgets. The rooms are clean and spacious, and the hostel provides free Wi-Fi, a guest kitchen, and a common lounge area where guests can relax and socialize. The friendly staff are always ready to offer tips on exploring Leipzig on a budget. Sleepy Lion Hostel is ideal for those looking for a lively and affordable place to stay.

Five Elements Hostel Leipzig

Five Elements Hostel Leipzig is located in the trendy district of Südvorstadt, known for its vibrant nightlife and eclectic dining options. The hostel offers a range of accommodations, from shared dormitories to private rooms, all at reasonable prices. The facilities include free Wi-Fi, a guest kitchen, a bar, and a cozy common area. The hostel also organizes events and tours, providing guests with opportunities to explore the city and meet new people. The central location and welcoming atmosphere make Five Elements Hostel a great choice for budget travelers who want to experience Leipzig's youthful and dynamic side.

Hostel Multitude

Hostel Multitude, situated in the up-and-coming district of Plagwitz, offers a unique and budget-friendly accommodation experience. This hostel is known for its artistic vibe and eco-friendly practices. The rooms are stylishly decorated with recycled materials and vintage furniture, creating a cozy and creative atmosphere. Guests can choose from shared dormitories or private rooms, all featuring free Wi-Fi and comfortable bedding. The hostel has a communal kitchen, a bar, and a garden where guests can relax. Hostel Multitude is perfect for travelers who appreciate sustainability and a laid-back, artistic environment.

Leipzig's diverse range of budget-friendly accommodations ensures that every traveler can find a comfortable and affordable place to stay. Whether you prefer the amenities of an affordable hotel, the social atmosphere of a hostel, the personal touch of a guesthouse, or a unique and alternative lodging experience, Leipzig has something to offer. By choosing one of these budget-friendly options, you can enjoy all that Leipzig has to offer without compromising on comfort or experience.

Tips for Booking and Choosing Accommodation

Choosing the right accommodation is a critical part of any travel experience. It can significantly impact your comfort, convenience, and overall enjoyment of the trip. With a variety of options available, from luxury hotels to budget-friendly hostels, making an informed choice can sometimes feel overwhelming. This chapter provides practical tips and insights to help you navigate the process of booking and selecting accommodations that best suit your needs, preferences, and budget.

The first step in choosing the right accommodation is to clearly define your needs and preferences. Consider the following aspects:

Purpose of Travel: Are you traveling for leisure, business, or a special event? Business travelers might prioritize proximity to business districts or conference centers, while leisure travelers might look for accommodations near tourist attractions.

Budget: Establish your maximum amount that you are prepared to pay for lodging. This will guarantee that you keep within your means and help you reduce the number of possibilities available to you.

Travel Companions: Are you traveling alone, with a partner, family, or a group of friends? The number and type of travel companions can influence your choice. For example, families might prefer accommodations with extra space and family-friendly amenities, while solo travelers might opt for hostels or budget hotels.

Length of Stay: For shorter stays, a hotel might be more convenient, whereas for longer stays, serviced apartments or vacation rentals with kitchen facilities might be more economical and comfortable.

Preferred Amenities: Make a list of must-have amenities such as Wi-Fi, breakfast, parking, a fitness center, or a pool. Prioritize these amenities based on what will enhance your stay the most.

Researching Your Options
Once you have a clear idea of what you need, start researching your options.
Online Travel Agencies (OTAs): Websites like Booking.com, Expedia, and Agoda allow you to search for accommodations based on your criteria. They offer filters for price, location, amenities, and guest ratings, making it easier to find suitable options.

Hotel Websites: Visiting the official websites of hotels can provide more detailed information about their offerings and often include special deals or discounts not available on third-party sites.

Travel Forums and Review Sites: Websites like TripAdvisor and Lonely Planet's Thorn Tree forum offer user-generated reviews and recommendations. Reading reviews from other travelers can give you a better sense of the quality and service of different accommodations.

Social Media and Blogs:Travel bloggers and influencers often share their experiences and recommendations for accommodations. Instagram, YouTube, and travel blogs can provide personal insights and visuals that help you make an informed decision.

Evaluating Location
The location of your accommodation can greatly influence your travel experience. Here are some tips for evaluating and choosing the best location:

Proximity to Attractions:If you're visiting Leipzig for its cultural and historical attractions, choose accommodations that are within walking distance or a short public transit ride from key sites such as the Leipzig Opera, St. Nicholas Church, and the city center.

Accessibility:Consider how easy it is to access your accommodation from the airport, train station, or major highways. Look for places with good public transportation links if you don't plan to rent a car.

Neighborhood Vibe: Different neighborhoods offer different vibes and amenities. For example, the city center is bustling and convenient, while districts like Plagwitz offer a more artistic and laid-back atmosphere.

Safety: Research the safety of the neighborhood, especially if you'll be arriving late or traveling alone. Look for accommodations in well-lit, populated areas.

Reading Reviews and Ratings
Reading reviews and ratings from other travelers can provide valuable insights into what you can expect. Here are some tips for effectively using reviews:

Look for Patterns: Don't rely on a single review. Look for patterns in the feedback. If multiple guests mention the same positive or negative points, they are likely accurate reflections of the accommodation.

Special Considerations

Certain travelers may have specific needs that should be taken into account when booking accommodations:

Families: Look for family-friendly hotels that offer amenities like cribs, extra beds, kids' menus, and play areas. Consider suites or apartments with kitchen facilities for convenience.

Business Travelers: Prioritize hotels with business centers, meeting rooms, reliable Wi-Fi, and proximity to business districts or conference venues.

Pet Owners: If you're traveling with a pet, make sure the accommodation is pet-friendly. Check for any additional fees and nearby parks or walking areas.

Eco-Conscious Travelers: For those who prioritize sustainability, look for accommodations with eco-friendly practices such as energy-efficient lighting, recycling programs, and locally sourced food.

Making the Most of Your Stay

Once you've booked your accommodation, there are a few tips to ensure a smooth and enjoyable stay:

Confirm Your Reservation: A few days before your arrival, confirm your reservation directly with the hotel to avoid any potential issues.

Check-In and Check-Out Times: Be aware of the hotel's check-in and check-out times to plan your arrival and departure accordingly. If you need an early check-in or late check-out, contact the hotel in advance to arrange it.

Special Requests: If you have any special requests, such as a quiet room, specific bed type, or dietary requirements, inform the hotel ahead of time to ensure they can accommodate you.

Local Insights:Take advantage of the local knowledge of the hotel staff. They can provide valuable recommendations for dining, sightseeing, and hidden gems in the area.

Safety and Security: Keep your valuables secure, use the hotel safe if available, and be mindful of your surroundings, especially when traveling alone.

Choosing and booking the right accommodation is a crucial step in planning a successful trip. By understanding your needs, researching your options, and using strategic booking techniques, you can find the perfect place to stay that fits your budget and enhances your travel experience. Whether you're looking for luxury, comfort, or budget-friendly options, Leipzig offers a wide range of accommodations to suit every traveler's needs. With these tips in mind, you can confidently navigate the booking process and enjoy a memorable and comfortable stay in this vibrant city.

CHAPTER 4
CULINARY DELIGHTS AND
DINING EXPERIENCES

Local Cuisine and Popular Dishes

Leipzig, a city with a thriving current and a rich cultural past, provides a gastronomic experience as interesting and varied as its past. This German city, which is tucked away in the heart of Saxony, blends contemporary culinary innovations with classic Saxon flavours. This chapter will take us on a culinary tour of Leipzig, where we will learn about the regional specialties, well-liked meals, and distinctive tastes that make this city a food lover's dream come true.

Saxon cuisine is characterized by hearty, flavorful dishes that reflect the agricultural richness of the region. Rooted in the traditions of rural life, the food of Leipzig incorporates locally-sourced ingredients, seasonal vegetables, and a variety of meats. Saxon food is often described as comfort food, known for its generous portions and robust flavors. Before diving into specific dishes, it's important to understand the key ingredients that define Saxon cooking. Potatoes, cabbage, and root vegetables are staples, often featured in soups, stews, and side dishes. Pork and beef are the most common meats, though game meats like venison are also popular. Freshwater fish from the many rivers and lakes in Saxony also find their way into local cuisine.

Bread plays a significant role in Saxon meals, with dark rye bread and rolls being common accompaniments. Dairy products, particularly butter and cheese, are also frequently used, adding richness to many dishes.

Leipziger Allerlei
One of the most famous dishes to originate from Leipzig is Leipziger Allerlei, a vibrant vegetable medley that celebrates the bounty of the region's produce. Traditionally, this dish includes a mix of young peas, carrots, asparagus, morels, and crayfish, often garnished with a rich cream sauce. It's a springtime favorite, showcasing the freshness of seasonal vegetables. Over the years, variations of the dish have emerged, but the core idea remains the same: a colorful, flavorful celebration of local vegetables.

Sauerbraten
Sauerbraten is a quintessential German pot roast, and the Saxon version is particularly beloved. This dish involves marinating a cut of beef in a mixture of

vinegar, water, and spices for several days before slow-cooking it to tender perfection. The result is a succulent, tangy roast often served with red cabbage and potato dumplings. The marinade gives Sauerbraten its characteristic sour flavor, balanced beautifully by the sweetness of the accompanying side dishes.

Sächsische Kartoffelsuppe

Potato soup is a staple in many German households, and Sächsische Kartoffelsuppe (Saxon potato soup) is a comforting, hearty version that's particularly popular in Leipzig. This soup is made with potatoes, leeks, carrots, and celery, simmered together with broth and often enhanced with bacon or sausage. It's typically garnished with fresh parsley and served with crusty bread. The combination of creamy potatoes and savory meats makes this soup a beloved comfort food, perfect for cold winter days.

Quarkkäulchen

For those with a sweet tooth, Quarkkäulchen is a must-try Saxon delicacy. These sweet cheese pancakes are made with quark (a type of fresh cheese), potatoes, flour, eggs, and a touch of sugar. They are fried to a golden brown and dusted with powdered sugar, often served with apple sauce or fresh fruit. The unique combination of quark and potatoes gives these pancakes a distinctive texture and flavor, making them a delightful treat.

Leipziger Lerchen

A historical tidbit accompanies Leipziger Lerchen, a pastry that carries a name meaning "Leipzig larks." Originally, this name referred to a dish made from actual larks, but due to a bird protection law in the 19th century, the culinary focus shifted. Today's Leipziger Lerchen are small, round pastries filled with a mix of crushed almonds, nuts, and a dollop of jam, typically raspberry or strawberry. These pastries are a testament to Leipzig's ability to adapt and innovate, transforming an old tradition into a beloved sweet treat.

Leipzig's culinary scene is a delightful blend of tradition and innovation, offering a rich array of flavors that reflect the city's history and contemporary spirit. From hearty Saxon classics to modern twists on traditional dishes, there is something to satisfy every palate. Whether

Top Restaurants

For those who love food, Leipzig is a paradise for It. Its food scene, which features everything from traditional Saxon meals to cosmopolitan cuisine, is as colorful and varied as its history. This chapter delves into Leipzig's top restaurant, offering readers who are eager to find the city's culinary gem a comprehensive and immersive experience.

Leipzig's food scene is characterized by an array of dining options that cater to all tastes and preferences. However, one restaurant stands out, combining exceptional food, an inviting atmosphere, and a deep connection to the local culture: Auerbachs Keller.

Auerbachs Keller, located in the Mädler Passage, is not just a restaurant; it's an institution. Dating back to the 16th century, it has long been a cornerstone of Leipzig's cultural and social life. This establishment is famously associated with Johann Wolfgang von Goethe, who immortalized it in his seminal work, *Faust*. When you dine here, you are not just enjoying a meal; you are partaking in a historical narrative that has shaped the city. From the moment you step into Auerbachs Keller, you are transported back in time. The interior is a testament to Leipzig's rich history, with wooden beams, vintage furnishings, and murals depicting scenes from Goethe's Faust. Despite its historical roots, the restaurant seamlessly blends old-world charm with modern comfort. The staff, dressed in traditional attire, welcome guests with warm hospitality, ensuring an inviting and relaxed dining experience.

Auerbachs Keller's menu is a carefully curated selection of Saxon specialties and contemporary dishes. The chefs here take pride in using locally sourced ingredients, ensuring that each dish is fresh and flavorful.

Begin your culinary journey with the Saxon Potato Soup, a hearty and creamy delight that perfectly sets the stage for what's to come. Another popular choice is the Leipziger Allerlei, a traditional vegetable medley that includes young peas, carrots, asparagus, and morels, often served with crayfish.

For the main course, the Saxon Sauerbraten is a must-try. This pot roast, marinated in a blend of vinegar, water, and spices, is slow-cooked to perfection, resulting in tender, flavorful meat that melts in your mouth. Served with red cabbage and potato dumplings, it's a dish that embodies the essence of Saxon cuisine. Another standout is the Rinderroulade, or beef roulade. Thinly sliced beef is rolled with a filling of bacon, onions, and pickles, then braised until succulent. The dish is typically accompanied by gravy and seasonal vegetables, making for a comforting and satisfying meal.

Vegetarian and Vegan Options
Auerbachs Keller also caters to vegetarian and vegan diners. The Vegetarian Platter, featuring a variety of seasonal vegetables, grains, and legumes, is both wholesome and delicious. Vegan guests can enjoy dishes like Mushroom Stroganoff, which uses plant-based ingredients to recreate the classic Russian dish.

Desserts
No meal at Auerbachs Keller is complete without indulging in their delectable desserts. The Quarkkeulchen, a type of Saxon cottage cheese pancake, is served with applesauce and powdered sugar, offering a sweet and tangy finish to your meal. Another favorite is the Rote Grütze, a traditional red fruit pudding that is light yet satisfying.

Auerbachs Keller boasts an impressive selection of local and international wines, with a particular focus on German varieties. The knowledgeable staff can recommend the perfect pairing for your meal, enhancing the flavors of each dish. Additionally, the restaurant offers a range of local beers, including the renowned Leipzig Gose, a slightly sour wheat beer that has been brewed in the region since the 16th century.

Dining at Auerbachs Keller is an experience that goes beyond the food. The restaurant often hosts cultural events, such as live music performances and literary readings, creating a vibrant and dynamic atmosphere. These events provide an opportunity to immerse yourself in Leipzig's cultural scene while enjoying a memorable meal.

Auerbachs Keller is committed to accessibility and sustainability. The restaurant is wheelchair accessible and offers menus in multiple languages, ensuring that all guests feel welcome. Moreover, their emphasis on locally sourced ingredients and environmentally friendly practices reflects a dedication to sustainability, making it a responsible choice for conscientious diners.

In the heart of Leipzig, Auerbachs Keller stands as a beacon of culinary excellence and historical significance. It offers more than just a meal; it provides a journey through time, culture, and flavor. Whether you are a history buff, a food enthusiast, or simply looking for an unforgettable dining experience, Auerbachs Keller is the place to be.

Street Food and Local Eateries

East German metropolis Leipzig is well-known for its diverse and lively culinary scene in addition to its rich history and cultural legacy. Even while Leipzig is home to several upscale restaurants and quaint cafés, the real highlight of the city's culinary scene is found in its street food and neighbourhood eateries. Through a tour of some of Leipzig's most well-liked street food vendors and neighbourhood restaurants, this chapter will give you a taste of the mouthwatering, varied, and frequently unexpected tastes that characterise this eclectic city.

Street food in Leipzig is a melting pot of cultures and flavors. From traditional German sausages to international delicacies, the city's street food vendors provide a wide array of options that cater to every taste bud. The charm of street food lies not only in its affordability and convenience but also in the communal experience it fosters. Locals and visitors alike gather around food trucks, market stalls, and pop-up kitchens, creating a vibrant atmosphere filled with the aroma of freshly cooked food and the buzz of lively conversation.

1. Currywurst
No exploration of German street food would be complete without trying Currywurst. This iconic dish

consists of steamed and fried pork sausage, sliced into bite-sized pieces, and smothered in a tangy ketchup-based curry sauce. Often served with a side of crispy fries, Currywurst is a favorite among locals and a must-try for any visitor. Head to Curry Cult, a popular spot known for its flavorful and generously portioned Currywurst.

2. Langos

Originating from Hungary, Langos has become a beloved street food in Leipzig. This deep-fried flatbread is typically topped with garlic butter, sour cream, and grated cheese, though variations with sweet toppings like Nutella are also available. The combination of the crispy exterior and soft, chewy interior makes Langos an irresistible treat. Check out the Langos stand at the Leipzig Market Square for an authentic taste.

3. Falafel

Leipzig's diverse food scene includes a strong Middle Eastern influence, and falafel is a prime example of this. These deep-fried balls made from ground chickpeas, herbs, and spices are usually served in pita bread with fresh vegetables and a drizzle of tahini sauce. For some of the best falafel in town, visit Libo's Falafel, where the flavors are authentic, and the ingredients are always fresh.

4. Handbrot

A visit to Leipzig wouldn't be complete without trying Handbrot, a delectable bread roll filled with cheese and ham, then baked until golden brown. This Saxon specialty is often served with a dollop of sour cream and chives, making it a comforting and satisfying snack. Handbrotzeit is a well-known spot where you can savor this local favorite.

Local Eateries: Authentic Flavors and Warm Atmospheres

Beyond the street food, Leipzig boasts a plethora of local eateries that offer both traditional German cuisine and innovative dishes. These establishments provide a more relaxed dining experience where you can enjoy a hearty meal and soak in the city's unique ambiance.

1. Zill's Tunnel

For a truly local dining experience, Zill's Tunnel is a must-visit. This cozy eatery offers a variety of Saxon specialties, including Leipziger Allerlei, a vegetable dish featuring peas, carrots, asparagus, and morels, often served with crayfish. The friendly atmosphere and traditional decor make Zill's Tunnel a perfect place to enjoy a leisurely meal and immerse yourself in Leipzig's culinary heritage.

2. Kartoffelhaus No. 1

Potatoes are a staple in German cuisine, and Kartoffelhaus No. 1 celebrates this versatile ingredient in all its glory. From potato pancakes and potato soup to baked potatoes with a variety of toppings, this restaurant showcases the many ways potatoes can be prepared and enjoyed. The rustic interior and hearty portions make it a popular spot for both locals and tourists.

3. Die Rosteria

Specializing in Thuringian sausages, Die Rosteria is a beloved local eatery that offers a modern twist on a regional classic. The sausages are grilled to perfection and served with an array of sides, including sauerkraut and potato salad. The casual, laid-back atmosphere makes it an excellent choice for a quick, satisfying meal.

Leipzig's street food and local eateries offer a delicious and diverse culinary experience that reflects the city's vibrant culture and history. From savoring traditional German dishes to exploring international flavors, there's something to delight every palate.

Whether you're grabbing a quick bite from a food truck or enjoying a leisurely meal at a historic restaurant, the food scene in Leipzig promises to be a highlight of your visit. So, take a stroll through the bustling markets, engage with the friendly locals, and indulge in the many delectable offerings this dynamic city has to offer.

Local Wine Tasting Experiences in Leipzig

A thriving wine culture is also present in Leipzig, a bustling city known for its rich cultural history and active arts scene. Saxony's scenic surroundings notwithstanding, Leipzig provides a fantastic range of local wine tasting experiences that appeal to wine fans of all stripes. Leipzig's oenological attractiveness is defined by its main vineyards, wine bars, and tasting events, all of which are highlighted in this chapter's exploration of the city's rich wine culture.

To fully appreciate Leipzig's wine tasting experiences, it's essential to understand the broader viticultural context of Saxony. This region, one of Germany's smallest wine-growing areas, has a history of viticulture that dates back to the 12th century. The unique climatic conditions and diverse soils contribute to the distinct character of Saxon wines, particularly known for their elegance and aromatic complexity.

Saxony is predominantly known for its white wines, with Müller-Thurgau, Riesling, and Weißburgunder (Pinot Blanc) being the most prominent varieties. However, red varieties such as Spätburgunder (Pinot Noir) and Dornfelder are also cultivated, adding to the region's diverse wine portfolio. The wines from this area are often marked by their fresh acidity, mineral notes, and expressive fruit flavors.

While Leipzig itself does not host extensive vineyards, it is surrounded by notable wine regions that are easily accessible for day trips. The most prominent of these is the Saale-Unstrut wine region, located to the west of Leipzig. This area is characterized by its steep, terraced vineyards along the riverbanks, creating a stunning backdrop for wine tours and tastings.

1. Weingut Lützkendorf
One of the standout wineries in the Saale-Unstrut region is Weingut Lützkendorf. Known for its meticulous craftsmanship and dedication to quality, this family-run winery produces an impressive range of wines, from crisp Rieslings to robust red blends. Visitors to Weingut Lützkendorf can enjoy guided tours of the vineyards, learn about the winemaking process, and taste a curated selection of their finest offerings in the picturesque tasting room.

2. Winzervereinigung Freyburg-Unstrut
Another must-visit destination is the Winzervereinigung Freyburg-Unstrut, a cooperative winery that represents numerous local growers. This cooperative approach allows for a wide variety of wines that capture the essence of the region. The

expansive tasting room and welcoming atmosphere make it an ideal spot for visitors to explore different styles and flavors. The knowledgeable staff are always on hand to provide insights and recommendations, ensuring a memorable experience.

3. Weingut Zahn
Weingut Zahn, situated in the quaint town of Großheringen, offers an intimate wine tasting experience. This boutique winery focuses on producing small batches of high-quality wines, emphasizing sustainability and traditional methods. The charming setting, coupled with personalized tastings, makes it a perfect choice for those looking to delve deeper into the nuances of Saxon wines.

Wine Bars and Tasting Rooms in Leipzig
For those who prefer to stay within the city limits, Leipzig boasts an array of wine bars and tasting rooms that bring the regional wine experience to urban enthusiasts. These venues often feature a curated selection of local wines alongside international favorites, providing a comprehensive tasting journey.

1. Weinhandlung und Vinothek Connewitz
Located in the vibrant district of Connewitz, this wine shop and tasting room offers an extensive selection of wines from Saxony and beyond. The

knowledgeable staff are passionate about wine and are always eager to share their expertise. Regular tasting events and themed evenings allow visitors to explore different wine styles and pairings, creating a dynamic and educational experience.

2. Vinothek 1770
Vinothek 1770, situated in the heart of Leipzig, is renowned for its elegant ambiance and carefully curated wine list. The bar's historic setting, combined with a modern approach to wine tasting, makes it a favorite among locals and tourists alike. Guests can choose from a wide range of wines by the glass, enabling them to sample various varieties and vintages. The sommeliers here are skilled at guiding patrons through their selections, ensuring a personalized and enriching experience.

3. Enoteca da Vini
For those seeking an Italian twist on their wine tasting experience, Enoteca da Vini offers an exceptional blend of local and Italian wines. This cozy wine bar, located in the Plagwitz district, features a warm and inviting atmosphere. The emphasis on pairing wine with authentic Italian cuisine enhances the tasting experience, allowing guests to appreciate the interplay of flavors and textures.

Leipzig's wine culture is further enriched by a variety of wine tasting events and festivals held throughout the year. These gatherings provide an excellent opportunity to sample a broad spectrum of wines, meet winemakers, and immerse oneself in the city's vibrant oenological community.

Leipzig's local wine tasting experiences offer a captivating journey through the flavors and traditions of Saxony's viticultural heritage. Whether you're exploring the scenic vineyards of the Saale-Unstrut region, enjoying a curated selection at a stylish wine bar, or immersing yourself in the festive atmosphere of a wine event, Leipzig provides a rich tapestry of opportunities for wine enthusiasts. By embracing the city's diverse wine culture and taking advantage of the practical tips outlined in this chapter, you can create unforgettable memories and deepen your appreciation for the art of winemaking. So raise your glass and toast to the vibrant wine culture that makes Leipzig a truly unique destination for oenophiles.

CHAPTER 5
EXPLORING OUTDOORS
ACTIVITIES AND ADVENTURES

Cycling and Hiking in Auwald (Leipzig Riverside Forest)

Welcome to the enchanting world of Auwald, also known as the Leipzig Riverside Forest, where nature's wonders await your exploration. In this chapter, we'll delve into the joyous experience of cycling and hiking through this lush and vibrant forest, offering a gateway to adventure and serenity for all who venture within.

As you step into Auwald, a sense of tranquility envelops you, transporting you away from the hustle and bustle of city life into a realm of natural beauty. The forest stretches along the banks of the picturesque rivers White Elster, Parthe, and Pleiße, providing a haven for outdoor enthusiasts and nature lovers alike. Cycling through Auwald is a liberating experience, allowing you to immerse yourself fully in the sights, sounds, and scents of the forest. The well-maintained trails meander through dense woodlands, alongside tranquil rivers, and past vibrant meadows, offering a diverse range of landscapes to explore. As you pedal along the winding paths, you'll encounter a tapestry of flora and fauna, from towering oak and beech trees to delicate wildflowers and chirping songbirds. Keep your eyes peeled for glimpses of deer grazing in the distance or squirrels darting through the undergrowth – each moment a testament to the richness of nature's bounty.

Whether you're a seasoned cyclist or a novice rider, Auwald has something to offer for everyone. From leisurely family outings to adrenaline-fueled mountain biking adventures, the forest caters to all skill levels and preferences. So, dust off your bike, don your helmet, and prepare to embark on an unforgettable journey through this verdant paradise.

For those who prefer to take things at a slower pace, hiking in Auwald promises a journey of discovery and contemplation. Lace up your hiking boots, pack a picnic, and set forth along the labyrinthine trails that crisscross the forest floor. Each step brings you closer to nature, as you weave your way through sun-dappled glades, across babbling brooks, and beneath the canopy of ancient trees. Along the way, pause to admire the intricate beauty of a spider's web glistening with dew, or to listen to the melodious symphony of birdsong echoing through the trees. As you ascend gentle slopes and descend into secluded valleys, you'll feel a sense of connection with the natural world that surrounds you – a connection that rejuvenates the body, mind, and spirit. Whether you're seeking solitude and introspection or companionship and camaraderie, Auwald offers a sanctuary where all are welcome to wander and wonder. Cycling and hiking in Auwald offer a gateway to adventure, discovery, and rejuvenation in the heart of nature. Whether you're seeking the thrill of exploration or the solace of solitude, the Leipzig Riverside Forest beckons with open arms, inviting you to immerse yourself in its timeless beauty and boundless wonders. So, strap on your helmet, lace up your boots, and embark on a journey of a lifetime through this enchanting realm of natural splendor.

Boating on the Leipzig New Lake District

Leipzig New Lake District is a place where the shimmering waters beckon adventurers and water enthusiasts alike to embark on a journey of exploration and relaxation. In this chapter, we'll delve into the exhilarating experience of boating on these tranquil lakes, offering a unique perspective on the beauty and serenity of Leipzig's aquatic landscapes.

The Leipzig New Lake District is a sprawling network of picturesque lakes, formed from former open-pit mines that have been transformed into havens of natural beauty and recreation. With crystal-clear waters reflecting the blue skies above and lush greenery lining the shores, these lakes provide the perfect backdrop for a day of boating adventures.

Whether you prefer the tranquility of paddling a kayak or the thrill of speeding across the water in a motorboat, the Leipzig New Lake District offers a variety of options to suit every taste and skill level. So, gather your friends and family, pack a picnic, and set sail on an unforgettable aquatic journey.

For those seeking a more intimate and immersive experience on the water, kayaking and canoeing are ideal choices. Glide silently across the glassy surface of the lakes, surrounded by the sights and sounds of nature unfolding around you.

As you paddle along, you'll have the opportunity to explore hidden coves, navigate narrow channels, and observe the abundant wildlife that calls the Leipzig New Lake District home. Keep your eyes peeled for graceful swans gliding gracefully across the water, or colorful dragonflies flitting among the reeds – each moment a reminder of the natural wonders that abound in this aquatic paradise.

For those craving a more exhilarating experience, motorboating offers the perfect opportunity to satisfy your thirst for adventure. Feel the wind in your hair and the sun on your face as you speed across the open waters, leaving a trail of frothy white wake in your wake.

With miles of open waterways to explore, the Leipzig New Lake District is a playground for boating enthusiasts of all stripes. Whether you're racing against friends in a friendly regatta or simply cruising at a leisurely pace, the freedom of the open water beckons, promising endless possibilities for excitement and discovery.

Before setting out on your boating adventure in the Leipzig New Lake District, here are a few tips to ensure a safe and enjoyable experience:

1. Wear a Life Jacket: Always wear a properly fitting life jacket while boating, regardless of your swimming ability.

2. Know the Rules: Familiarize yourself with local boating regulations and safety guidelines before hitting the water.

3. Check the Weather: Keep an eye on the weather forecast and avoid boating in inclement conditions.

4. Respect Wildlife: Observe wildlife from a safe distance and avoid disturbing their natural habitats.

Boating on the Leipzig New Lake District offers a unique opportunity to connect with nature, unwind from the stresses of daily life, and create lasting memories with friends and loved ones. Whether you're paddling serenely across the water in a kayak or racing against the wind in a motorboat, the beauty and tranquility of Leipzig's lakes are sure to captivate your heart and soul. So, hoist your sails, grab your paddles, and set forth on a voyage of discovery and adventure across the pristine waters of the Leipzig New Lake District. Fair winds and following seas await!

Climbing at K4 Kletterfelsen

Prepare for an exhilarating odyssey into the realm of rock climbing at K4 Kletterfelsen! This chapter unveils the adrenaline-fueled experience of ascending the awe-inspiring walls of this climbing sanctuary. Whether you're a novice or a seasoned climber, K4 Kletterfelsen offers an abundance of challenges and victories. So, gear up, chalk your hands, and let's embark on this thrilling adventure together!

1. Getting Started

Before you begin your ascent, it's essential to familiarize yourself with the climbing area. K4 Kletterfelsen boasts a variety of routes, each marked with different colors indicating its difficulty level. Start with a route that matches your skill level, and gradually work your way up as you gain confidence and strength.

2. Safety First

Safety is paramount in rock climbing, and K4 Kletterfelsen prioritizes it above all else. Before you take your first step, ensure that your harness is properly secured, your knots are tied correctly, and your climbing partner is ready to belay you. Remember to communicate effectively with your partner throughout the climb, using clear signals and commands to ensure a safe and enjoyable experience for both of you.

3. Technique Tips
Both skill and strength are important factors in climbing. As you navigate the walls of K4 Kletterfelsen, pay attention to your footwork, body positioning, and hand placements. Instead of using just your arms, raise yourself up by using your legs. Keep your hips close to the wall to maintain balance, and use your hands to grip the holds with precision and control.

4. Overcoming Challenges
Climbing at K4 Kletterfelsen will undoubtedly present you with challenges along the way. Whether it's a particularly tricky move or a daunting overhang, approach each obstacle with determination and a positive mindset. Break the route down into smaller, manageable sections, and focus on making steady progress one step at a time. Remember, it's okay to take breaks and reassess your strategy if needed.

5. Enjoying the View
As you ascend higher and higher, don't forget to pause and take in the breathtaking views that K4 Kletterfelsen has to offer. From your vantage point on the wall, you'll be treated to sweeping vistas of

lush greenery, jagged cliffs, and the vast expanse of the sky above. Take a moment to appreciate the beauty of nature and the sense of accomplishment that comes with conquering each new height.

6. Pushing Your Limits

Once you've mastered the easier routes, it's time to push yourself out of your comfort zone and tackle more challenging climbs. K4 Kletterfelsen provides plenty of opportunities for growth and development, with routes of varying difficulty levels to test your skills and push your limits. Embrace the challenge, embrace the adrenaline, and embrace the thrill of pushing yourself to new heights.

7. Reflecting on Your Journey

As you descend back to solid ground, take a moment to reflect on your climbing journey at K4 Kletterfelsen. Celebrate your achievements, no matter how small, and acknowledge the progress you've made since your first climb. Consider the lessons you've learned along the way – about perseverance, resilience, and the power of self-belief – and carry them with you as you continue your climbing adventures beyond the walls of K4 Kletterfelsen.

climbing at K4 Kletterfelsen is an experience like no other – a journey of discovery, challenge, and exhilaration that will leave you feeling empowered and inspired. So, grab your gear, lace up your shoes, and join us as we reach new heights together at K4 Kletterfelsen!

Adventure Awaits at Leipzig
Kletterwald Leipzig

Step into the exhilarating world of Adventure Park Leipzig, also known as Kletterwald Leipzig! Located in the heart of Leipzig, this thrilling destination offers a haven for adventure seekers of all ages. From soaring through the treetops to conquering challenging obstacles, every moment at Kletterwald Leipzig promises excitement, discovery, and unforgettable memories.

Readiness for embarking on an incredible journey? At Adventure Park Leipzig, adventure awaits around every corner. As you step into the lush forest surroundings, you'll feel a rush of anticipation and excitement. With a variety of courses ranging from easy to challenging, there's something for everyone, whether you're a beginner or a seasoned adventurer.

Get ready to test your skills and push your limits on our thrilling courses. Each course is carefully designed to provide a unique and exciting experience, featuring a combination of ziplines, rope bridges, and obstacles to overcome. Whether you're navigating through the canopy or traversing obstacles suspended high above the ground, you'll be surrounded by breathtaking natural beauty every step of the way.

-Beginner Courses: Perfect for first-time climbers and families, our beginner courses offer a gentle introduction to the world of treetop adventure. Navigate through low-hanging obstacles and zip lines while building confidence and mastering the basics of climbing and balance.

Intermediate Courses: Ready to take your adventure to the next level? Our intermediate courses offer a mix of moderate challenges and adrenaline-pumping thrills. Test your agility as you tackle elevated obstacles and zip lines, with plenty of opportunities to push yourself and conquer new heights.

Advanced Courses: For the ultimate thrill-seekers, our advanced courses provide a true test of skill and courage. Navigate through a series of challenging obstacles and zip lines, including high-speed descents and heart-pounding crossings. Are you up for the challenge?

At Adventure Park Leipzig, safety is our top priority. Before you embark on your adventure, our experienced guides will provide thorough safety instructions and ensure that you're properly equipped with harnesses and helmets. Throughout your climb, our trained staff will be on hand to offer assistance and guidance, ensuring that you can focus on having fun while staying safe.

Looking for a fun-filled day out with the family? Adventure Park Leipzig is the perfect destination for adventurers of all ages. Whether you're celebrating a birthday, planning a family outing, or looking for a unique team-building experience, our park offers something for everyone. With courses designed specifically for children and adults, there's no better way to bond with your loved ones while enjoying the great outdoors.

Ready to experience the thrill of Adventure Park Leipzig? The following information will help you organise your visit:

Location: Adventure Park Leipzig is located in the beautiful Leipzig Forest, just a short drive from the city center. With easy access by car or public transportation, getting here is a breeze.

Opening Hours: Our park is open year-round, with varying hours depending on the season. Be sure to check our website for the latest information on opening times and special events.

Tickets: Admission to Adventure Park Leipzig includes access to all of our courses, as well as equipment rental and safety instruction. Discounts are available for groups, students, and seniors, making it easy to enjoy a day of adventure without breaking the bank. What to Bring: Be sure to wear comfortable clothing and closed-toe shoes suitable for outdoor activity. Don't forget to bring a sense of adventure and a camera to capture all of the unforgettable moments! As you embark on your adventure at Adventure Park Leipzig, prepare to be amazed, challenged, and inspired. Whether you're conquering obstacles, soaring through the treetops, or simply enjoying the beauty of nature, every moment spent at Kletterwald Leipzig is an opportunity for adventure and discovery. So gather your friends and family, embrace the thrill of the unknown, and let the adventure begin!

Bird Watching in the Leipzig Floodplain Forest

Bird watching, or birding, is a delightful way to connect with nature, offering a peaceful escape from the bustle of everyday life. The Leipzig Floodplain Forest, known as the Auwald, provides an exceptional setting for this pursuit. Nestled along the Elster, Pleiße, and Luppe rivers, this ancient forest is a biodiverse haven, teeming with avian life. Whether you are a seasoned birder or a curious beginner, the Auwald presents a perfect backdrop for discovering a wide array of bird species.

The Leipzig Floodplain Forest is one of the largest continuous floodplain forests in Central Europe. This unique ecosystem supports a diverse range of habitats, including dense woodlands, wetlands, and open meadows, each offering different opportunities for bird watching. The varied landscape attracts a plethora of bird species, making it a prime location for birders. In the Auwald, you can expect to encounter everything from common garden birds to rare and migratory species. The forest's seasonal changes also mean that each visit can reveal new avian surprises. Spring and autumn, in particular, are peak times for bird watching, as migratory birds pass through the region.

Before heading into the forest, it's important to be well-prepared. Here are some essentials for a successful bird watching adventure:

1. Binoculars: A good pair of binoculars is indispensable. Look for ones with a magnification of at least 8x to 10x.
2. Field Guide: A bird identification guide specific to Central Europe will help you recognize different species.
3. Notebook and Pen: Keeping a birding journal allows you to record sightings, behaviors, and any other notes.
4. Camera: For those interested in bird photography, a camera with a good zoom lens is ideal.
5. Appropriate Clothing: Wear weather-appropriate, neutral-colored clothing to blend into the environment and avoid startling the birds.
6. Comfortable Footwear: Sturdy walking shoes or boots are essential for navigating the often muddy and uneven forest trails.

Seasonal Bird Watching in the Auwald
The bird population in the Auwald changes with the seasons, offering unique experiences throughout the year:

Spring: This is the best time for bird watching, as migratory birds return to the forest. Look for breeding pairs and listen for elaborate mating songs.

Summer: Many birds are busy feeding their young, providing opportunities to observe family groups. The dense foliage can make spotting birds more challenging, but rewarding.

Autumn: As birds prepare for migration, the forest comes alive with activity. This is a great time to see large flocks of birds gathering.

Winter: Although bird activity slows down, the Auwald still hosts several resident species. Woodpeckers, tits, and nuthatches are commonly seen during this season.

Bird Conservation in the Auwald

The Leipzig Floodplain Forest is not just a birding paradise but also a critical area for bird conservation. Efforts are made to preserve and restore habitats, ensuring that the forest remains a sanctuary for birdlife.

Organizations and local conservationists work tirelessly to monitor bird populations and protect breeding sites. Public awareness campaigns and educational programs help foster a sense of responsibility among visitors and locals alike. By respecting the forest and following guidelines, bird watchers contribute to these conservation efforts.

Bird Watching Etiquette

Respect for the environment and wildlife is paramount when bird watching. Here are some guidelines to follow:

1. Keep Your Distance: Avoid getting too close to birds, especially during the breeding season when they are most vulnerable.
2. Stay on Paths: Stick to designated trails to minimize habitat disturbance.
3. Leave No Trace: Carry out all litter and be mindful of your impact on the environment.
4. Respect Other Birders: Be considerate of fellow bird watchers by keeping noise to a minimum and sharing observations politely.
5. Report Sightings: Contributing to citizen science projects by reporting rare or unusual sightings can aid conservation efforts.

Bird watching offers numerous benefits beyond the joy of spotting birds. It is a meditative activity that promotes mindfulness and reduces stress. The gentle rhythm of nature and the focus required to observe birds can be profoundly calming. Studies have shown that spending time in nature improves mental health, boosts mood, and enhances overall well-being. Bird watching, in particular, encourages you to slow down, breathe deeply, and engage fully with your surroundings.

Bird watching in the Leipzig Floodplain Forest is an enriching experience that combines the beauty of nature with the thrill of discovery. Whether you're marveling at the sight of a white stork in flight or listening to the melodic song of a nightingale, the Auwald offers endless opportunities for connection with the natural world. By preparing well, respecting wildlife, and embracing the serenity of the forest, bird watchers can enjoy countless rewarding moments. The Auwald stands as a testament to the wonders of biodiversity and the importance of preserving such precious habitats for future generations to explore and cherish.

Horseback Riding Adventure

Are you prepared to set out on a unique adventure?? Picture yourself astride a majestic horse, wind in your hair, exploring the beautiful countryside of Leipzig. Whether you're a seasoned rider or someone who's always dreamt of saddling up, horseback riding in Leipzig offers an experience that's both exhilarating and unforgettable.

Horseback riding isn't just a hobby; it's a passion that connects us with nature and with these magnificent creatures. In Leipzig, surrounded by rolling hills, picturesque forests, and tranquil lakes, the stage is set for an unforgettable equestrian adventure.

Leipzig's countryside is a patchwork of breathtaking landscapes just waiting to be explored on horseback. Imagine riding through verdant meadows adorned with wildflowers, along winding trails that lead through ancient forests, and beside sparkling lakes that reflect the sky like mirrors. Whether you're a nature lover, a thrill-seeker, or simply someone who enjoys the freedom of the open road, Leipzig's countryside has something to offer everyone.

Before you can hit the trails, you'll need to find the right riding stable to suit your needs. Luckily, Leipzig is home to several reputable stables that offer a range of riding experiences for riders of all levels. Whether you're looking for a leisurely trail ride, a challenging hack through the wilderness, or even lessons to improve your riding skills, there's a stable out there for you.

One such stable is Reitstall Am Wasserturm, a family-run establishment located just outside Leipzig. Here, you'll find friendly instructors, well-trained horses, and scenic trails that wind through the surrounding countryside. Whether you're a beginner or an experienced rider, Reitstall Am Wasserturm has something to offer everyone.

Before you saddle up, it's important to have the right gear and attire. Safety should always be your top priority when horseback riding, so be sure to invest in a properly fitted riding helmet to protect your head in case of falls or accidents. You'll also need sturdy riding boots with a low heel to provide stability and protection, as well as comfortable clothing that allows for ease of movement. Don't forget gloves to protect your hands and sunscreen to shield yourself from the sun's rays.

Horseback riding is a thrilling and rewarding experience, but it's important to remember that it also comes with its own set of risks. Before mounting your horse, take the time to familiarize yourself with basic riding etiquette and safety guidelines. Always listen to your instructor and follow their instructions carefully, and be sure to maintain control of your horse at all times. Stay alert and aware of your surroundings, and be respectful of other riders and trail users.

Once you're geared up and ready to go, it's time to hit the trails and explore Leipzig's stunning countryside on horseback. Whether you're riding through the Leipzig Floodplain Forest, circling the shores of Cospudener See, or venturing into the Mulde River Valley, there's no shortage of breathtaking landscapes to discover. So saddle up, take the reins, and let the adventure begin!

Horseback riding isn't just about the thrill of the ride; it's about forging a bond with these magnificent animals and experiencing the beauty of nature in a whole new way. Whether you're trotting through a sun-dappled forest, cantering across an open meadow, or simply enjoying the rhythmic beat of your horse's hooves beneath you, there's something truly magical about the experience.

Horseback riding in Leipzig offers a unique opportunity to connect with nature, explore stunning landscapes, and experience the thrill of riding a horse. Whether you're a seasoned equestrian or someone who's always dreamt of saddling up, there's never been a better time to discover the joys of horseback riding in Leipzig. So why wait? Saddle up, take the reins, and let the adventure begin!

Swimming and Relaxing at Cospudener See

Discover the tranquil beauty of Cospudener See, a haven for swimmers, sunbathers, and nature lovers alike. Located in the Leipzig Neuseenland region, this stunning lake offers crystal-clear waters, sandy beaches, and lush greenery, providing the perfect backdrop for a day of swimming and relaxation. Join me as we dive into the refreshing waters of Cospudener See and embrace the serenity of its shores.

Arriving at Cospudener See, I was immediately captivated by its natural allure. The shimmering blue waters stretched out before me, beckoning me to immerse myself in their refreshing embrace. Finding a secluded spot on the sandy beach, I spread out my towel and eagerly made my way to the water's edge.

Stepping into the cool, clear waters of Cospudener See was like stepping into a sanctuary of tranquility. The gentle lapping of the waves against the shore, the warmth of the sun on my skin, and the sensation of weightlessness as I floated effortlessly in the water all combined to create a sense of pure bliss.

For hours, I swam and splashed around, reveling in the freedom and exhilaration of being surrounded by nature's beauty. As I explored further from the shore, I marveled at the underwater world beneath me, where sunlight danced on the sandy bottom and colorful fish darted playfully through the water.

After a refreshing swim, I retreated to the shore to bask in the sun's warm rays. Stretching out on my towel, I closed my eyes and let the gentle breeze caress my skin, allowing myself to fully relax and unwind in this idyllic paradise.

Cospudener See offers an ideal setting for swimming, with its clean, clear waters and designated swimming areas ensuring a safe and enjoyable experience for all. Whether you're seeking a leisurely dip near the shore or a more adventurous swim further out, the lake caters to swimmers of all abilities.

As I ventured deeper into the water, I discovered that Cospudener See offers something for everyone. For those looking for a peaceful swim, the calm waters near the shore provide a serene environment to relax and unwind. For the more adventurous, the deeper areas of the lake offer ample opportunities for exploration and excitement.

Safety is paramount when swimming at Cospudener See, with lifeguards patrolling the designated swimming areas to ensure the well-being of all visitors. By adhering to any posted safety guidelines and swimming within the designated boundaries, you can enjoy a worry-free day on the water.

In addition to its inviting waters, Cospudener See boasts several sandy beaches and grassy areas where visitors can relax and soak up the sun. Whether you prefer to lounge on a towel, sit in a beach chair, or picnic on the grass, there are plenty of tranquil spots to enjoy the scenery and unwind.

As I reclined on the shore, I was enveloped by a sense of peace and serenity. The rhythmic sound of the waves, the gentle rustle of the leaves, and the distant laughter of fellow beachgoers all contributed to a feeling of utter contentment. It was the perfect opportunity to escape the stresses of daily life and reconnect with the natural world.

Beyond swimming and sunbathing, Cospudener See offers a variety of activities and amenities to enhance your experience. From kayaking and paddleboarding to beach volleyball and yoga, there's something for everyone to enjoy. Beachside cafes and snack bars provide refreshments, while shops and rental facilities offer everything you need for a day at the lake.

As responsible visitors to Cospudener See, it's important to respect and protect the natural environment. Avoid littering or leaving behind any trash, and be mindful of wildlife and vegetation. By practicing Leave No Trace principles and respecting the lake's ecosystem, we can ensure that Cospudener See remains a pristine and enjoyable destination for years to come. Swimming and relaxing at Cospudener See is more than just a pastime – it's a rejuvenating experience that nourishes the body, mind, and soul. Whether you're seeking adventure on the water or simply looking to unwind on the shore, Cospudener See offers a sanctuary of tranquility amidst the beauty of nature.

CHAPTER 6

IMMERSING IN THE ARTS, CULTURE, AND ENTERTAINMENT

Celebrating Community Local Festivals and Events

Explore Leipzig's dynamic cultural scene through its lively festivals and events that unite the community in celebration. From literary gatherings to music festivals, culinary delights to seasonal markets, Leipzig offers a diverse array of experiences to suit every taste and interest. Join us as we delve into the vibrant tapestry of local culture and discover the unique spirit that makes Leipzig's festivals truly unforgettable.

The Heartbeat of Leipzig: Festivals and Events
Leipzig is a city that knows how to throw a party, and its calendar is filled with a colorful array of festivals and events throughout the year. From traditional celebrations rooted in centuries-old customs to modern gatherings that push the boundaries of creativity, there's something for everyone to enjoy. Whether you're a music lover, a foodie, or an art

enthusiast, Leipzig's festivals offer an opportunity to experience the city's vibrant culture and connect with its diverse community.

Leipzig Book Fair
Every spring, bookworms from around the world flock to Leipzig for one of the largest and most prestigious book fairs in Europe. The Leipzig Book Fair is a celebration of literature, where authors, publishers, and book enthusiasts come together to explore the latest literary offerings, attend readings and lectures, and meet their favorite writers. From bestsellers to hidden gems, the fair showcases the rich diversity of the publishing world and offers a glimpse into the literary landscape of today and tomorrow.

Wave-Gotik-Treffen: Where Gothic Culture Flourishes
For fans of alternative music and subculture, Wave-Gotik-Treffen is an unmissable event that takes place every year during the Pentecost weekend. This unique festival celebrates gothic culture in all its forms, featuring live music performances, art exhibitions, film screenings, and elaborate costumes that transform Leipzig into a playground of darkness and decadence. Whether you're a die-hard goth or simply curious to explore this fascinating subculture, Wave-Gotik-Treffen offers an unforgettable experience unlike any other.

Bachfest Leipzig

As the birthplace of Johann Sebastian Bach, Leipzig pays homage to its most famous son with an annual festival dedicated to his life and music. Bachfest Leipzig brings together world-class musicians, choirs, and orchestras to perform Bach's masterpieces in historic venues across the city. From grand concerts in churches and concert halls to intimate chamber music recitals, the festival offers a chance to experience the timeless beauty and genius of Bach's music in the very city where he lived and worked.

Leipzig Christmas Market: A Winter Wonderland

When the holiday season arrives, Leipzig transforms into a magical winter wonderland with its enchanting Christmas market. Dating back over 500 years, the Leipzig Christmas Market is one of the oldest and largest in Germany, attracting visitors with its festive atmosphere, twinkling lights, and charming wooden stalls selling traditional crafts, seasonal treats, and mulled wine. From ice skating on the market square to listening to carolers sing in the glow of candlelight, the Leipzig Christmas Market is a cherished tradition that brings joy and warmth to locals and visitors alike.

Street Food Festival: A Culinary Adventure
For foodies craving a taste of global cuisine, Leipzig's Street Food Festival is a culinary extravaganza not to be missed. Held several times a year at various locations throughout the city, the festival brings together food trucks, pop-up stalls, and local vendors serving up a mouthwatering array of international street food delights. From gourmet burgers and sushi rolls to vegan tacos and decadent desserts, there's no shortage of delicious dishes to tempt your taste buds. With live music, cooking demonstrations, and a lively atmosphere, the Street Food Festival is a feast for the senses that celebrates the diversity of Leipzig's culinary scene.

From literary enthusiasts to music aficionados, food lovers to cultural connoisseurs, Leipzig's festivals and events offer something for everyone to enjoy. Whether you're exploring the latest literary offerings at the Book Fair, immersing yourself in gothic culture at Wave-Gotik-Treffen, or savoring the flavors of the world at the Street Food Festival, you'll find yourself swept up in the vibrant energy and rich cultural fabric of this dynamic city. So mark your calendars, gather your friends and family, and get ready to celebrate the spirit of Leipzig at its finest!

Art Galleries and Museums

Leipzig's cultural scene extends beyond festivals and events to include a wealth of art galleries and museums that showcase the city's rich history, artistic heritage, and contemporary creativity. In this chapter, we'll delve into the diverse array of galleries and museums that Leipzig has to offer, from renowned institutions to hidden gems waiting to be discovered. Whether you're a seasoned art enthusiast or simply curious to explore, Leipzig's galleries and museums promise an enriching and inspiring experience for visitors of all backgrounds.

The Leipzig School: A Legacy of Artistic Excellence
Leipzig has long been associated with artistic innovation and creativity, thanks in part to the illustrious Leipzig School of Art. Founded in the 18th century, the Leipzig School has produced some of Germany's most celebrated artists, including Max Beckmann, Otto Dix, and Neo Rauch. Today, the legacy of the Leipzig School lives on in the city's thriving art scene, where emerging talents and established artists alike continue to push the boundaries of artistic expression.

The Fine Arts Museum, also known as the Museum of Bildenden Künste
One of Leipzig's premier cultural institutions, the Museum of Fine Arts is home to an extensive collection of European art spanning from the Middle Ages to the present day. With over 7,000 works on display, including paintings, sculptures, and decorative arts, the museum offers a comprehensive overview of Western art history. Highlights of the collection include masterpieces by Lucas Cranach the Elder, Caspar David Friedrich, and Auguste Rodin, as well as contemporary works by artists such as Neo Rauch and Rosa Loy.

The Grassi Museum Complex
Comprising three separate museums – the Museum of Applied Arts, the Museum of Ethnography, and the Museum of Musical Instruments – the Grassi Museum Complex offers a fascinating journey through human creativity and cultural diversity. From exquisite porcelain and decorative arts to artifacts from around the world and a vast collection of musical instruments, the museums provide insight into the artistic, cultural, and musical traditions of Leipzig and beyond.

The Spinnerei: A Hub of Contemporary Art
Once a sprawling cotton mill, the Spinnerei has been transformed into a vibrant center for contemporary

art and culture. Today, the complex is home to over 100 artist studios, galleries, and cultural spaces, making it one of the largest and most dynamic art communities in Europe. Visitors to the Spinnerei can explore a wide range of artistic practices, from painting and sculpture to photography, video, and installation art, and engage directly with artists working in their studios.

The Leipzig Museum of Contemporary Art (Galerie für Zeitgenössische Kunst)

Dedicated to showcasing the latest developments in contemporary art, the Leipzig Museum of Contemporary Art (Galerie für Zeitgenössische Kunst) is a must-visit for art enthusiasts seeking to explore cutting-edge artistic practices. With a diverse program of exhibitions, events, and educational initiatives, the museum provides a platform for emerging artists and established practitioners alike to engage with contemporary issues and ideas.

From the historic masterpieces of the Museum of Fine Arts to the cutting-edge contemporary art of the Spinnerei, Leipzig's art galleries and museums offer a captivating journey through the city's cultural heritage and creative spirit.

Whether you're marveling at Old Masters or discovering the next generation of artistic talent, Leipzig's galleries and museums promise an enriching and inspiring experience for visitors of all ages and interests. So come explore the city's vibrant cultural landscape and discover the artistry that lies at the heart of Leipzig's identity.

Exploring Shopping and Markets

In Leipzig, shopping isn't just about acquiring goods; it's an immersive experience that reflects the city's dynamic culture and diverse offerings. From historic marketplaces to modern shopping districts, Leipzig boasts a wide range of retail destinations that cater to every taste and budget. Join us as we explore the city's vibrant shopping scene, uncovering hidden gems, local treasures, and unforgettable experiences along the way.

Historic Marketplaces: Where History Meets Commerce

Step back in time and experience Leipzig's rich history at its historic marketplaces. The Marktplatz, located in the heart of the city, has been a hub of commerce and social activity for centuries. Here, you'll find the iconic Altes Rathaus (Old Town Hall) and the imposing Alte Börse (Old Stock Exchange), as well as a bustling market where vendors sell fresh produce, artisanal goods, and souvenirs.

Another must-visit destination is the Naschmarkt, Leipzig's oldest market square. Dating back to the 16th century, the Naschmarkt is famous for its traditional delicacies, including local specialties like Leipziger Lerche (a pastry filled with marzipan and jam) and Leipziger Allerlei (a vegetable dish with asparagus, peas, carrots, and more).

Shopping Districts: Where Fashion and Style Collide

For those in search of the latest trends and designer labels, Leipzig's shopping districts offer an array of upscale boutiques and department stores. The city center is home to renowned shopping streets like the Grimmaische Straße and the Petersstraße, where you'll find high-end fashion brands, luxury retailers, and chic boutiques catering to discerning shoppers.

If you're looking for something a bit more eclectic, head to the Südvorstadt district, known for its vibrant mix of vintage shops, indie boutiques, and quirky stores. Here, you can browse for unique clothing, accessories, and home decor items while soaking in the neighborhood's bohemian charm.

Leipzig is full of hidden gems waiting to be discovered, from tucked-away boutiques to off-the-beaten-path markets. Take a stroll down the Karl-Liebknecht-Straße, a bustling street lined with independent shops, cafes, and art galleries. Here, you'll find everything from handmade jewelry and artisanal crafts to vintage vinyl records and antique books.

For a taste of local culture and creativity, don't miss the Baumwollspinnerei (Cotton Mill), a former industrial complex that has been transformed into a vibrant arts and culture center. Here, you can explore artist studios, galleries, and shops showcasing contemporary art, design, and fashion from Leipzig and beyond.

Markets and Flea Markets: A Treasure Trove of Bargains

No visit to Leipzig is complete without a trip to one of its markets or flea markets, where you can haggle for bargains, sample local delicacies, and soak up the lively atmosphere. The Leipzig Hauptbahnhof (central train station) hosts a weekly farmers' market, where you can stock up on fresh produce, artisanal cheeses, and baked goods from local farmers and producers.

For vintage lovers and bargain hunters, the Leipzig Antikmeile (Antique Mile) is a paradise of retro treasures and secondhand finds. Here, you can browse for vintage clothing, antique furniture, collectibles, and more, while enjoying live music, street food, and entertainment.

Shopping and markets in Leipzig are more than just transactions; they're opportunities to explore the city's rich history, vibrant culture, and creative spirit. Whether you're browsing for designer labels in the city center, uncovering hidden gems in independent boutiques, or haggling for bargains at flea markets, Leipzig offers a shopping experience like no other. So grab your bags, lace up your shoes, and get ready to shop 'til you drop in this dynamic and diverse city.

Nightlife and Entertainment Options

When the sun sets in Leipzig, the city comes alive with an electrifying energy that pulses through its streets and venues. From trendy bars and clubs to cultural hotspots and live music venues, Leipzig's nightlife scene offers something for everyone to enjoy. Join us as we explore the diverse array of nighttime entertainment options that make Leipzig a destination for revelers and night owls alike.

Bars and Pubs: Toasting to Good Times

Leipzig's bar scene is as diverse as it is vibrant, with establishments ranging from cozy pubs and historic taverns to sleek cocktail bars and trendy lounges. Start your evening with a pint of local beer at one of the city's traditional pubs, where you can mingle with locals and soak up the atmosphere of Leipzig's historic neighborhoods.

For a more upscale experience, head to one of Leipzig's cocktail bars, where skilled mixologists craft innovative drinks using premium spirits and fresh ingredients. From classic cocktails to creative concoctions, these bars offer a sophisticated setting to sip and socialize with friends.

Clubs and Dance Floors: Keeping the Party Going

When it's time to hit the dance floor, Leipzig's club scene delivers an unforgettable nightlife experience. Whether you're into techno, house, hip-hop, or indie music, there's a club for every taste and style. Dance the night away to pulsating beats and cutting-edge sounds at one of Leipzig's renowned clubs, where top DJs and live acts keep the party going until the early hours of the morning.

For those who prefer a more intimate setting, Leipzig is home to a thriving underground scene with hidden clubs and pop-up parties that cater to music lovers and night owls looking for a unique and immersive experience.

Live Music Venues: Rocking Out to the Beat

If live music is more your speed, Leipzig has you covered with a vibrant array of venues showcasing local bands, international acts, and everything in between. From intimate jazz clubs and cozy cafes to larger concert halls and outdoor amphitheaters, there's no shortage of options for catching a live performance in Leipzig. For a taste of the city's indie music scene, check out one of Leipzig's underground venues or DIY spaces, where up-and-coming bands and artists take the stage and showcase their talent to enthusiastic crowds. Or, for a more mainstream experience, head to one of the city's larger venues, where you can catch chart-topping acts and established musicians performing to packed houses.

Cultural Hotspots: Nourishing the Mind and Soul

Beyond bars and clubs, Leipzig offers a wealth of cultural hotspots and entertainment options for those looking to nourish their minds and souls. From art galleries and theaters to cinemas and performance spaces, there's always something happening in Leipzig's cultural scene. Catch a play at one of Leipzig's renowned theaters, where talented actors and directors bring classic works and contemporary productions to life on stage. Or, explore the city's thriving arts scene at one of its many galleries and exhibition spaces, where you can discover cutting-edge contemporary art, photography, and more.

Leipzig's nightlife and entertainment options are as diverse and dynamic as the city itself, offering something for every taste and interest. Whether you're looking to dance the night away at a club, catch a live performance at a music venue, or explore the city's cultural offerings, Leipzig promises an unforgettable experience for night owls and revelers alike. So grab your friends, hit the town, and get ready to make memories that will last a lifetime in this vibrant and bustling city after dark.

CHAPTER 7
A WEEKLONG ADVENTURE

Day 1
Arrival and Discovery in Leipzig

Leipzig is a city where history meets modernity, and culture thrives at every corner. Today marks the beginning of your adventure in this vibrant city, where each street and square has a story to tell and every experience is a journey of discovery. So, let's embark on this exciting day together, filled with exploration, immersion, and unforgettable moments.

Morning: Arrival in Leipzig
As the sun rises on the horizon, you find yourself arriving in Leipzig, filled with anticipation and excitement for the adventures that lie ahead. Whether you're arriving by plane, train, or car, the journey to Leipzig is part of the experience, offering glimpses of the city's picturesque landscapes and vibrant neighborhoods as you approach your destination.

Upon arrival, take a moment to breathe in the crisp morning air and soak in the energy of the city. Leipzig's welcoming atmosphere and friendly locals make you feel right at home from the moment you step foot on its streets. If you're arriving by train, the historic Leipzig Hauptbahnhof welcomes you with its grandeur and charm, while the bustling airport provides a gateway to the city's wonders.

Late Morning: Checking In and Refreshing
After your journey, it's time to check in to your accommodation and freshen up before beginning your day of exploration. Leipzig offers a range of accommodations to suit every taste and budget, from boutique hotels in the city center to cozy guesthouses in the suburbs. Take some time to settle in, unpack your bags, and recharge your batteries for the adventures ahead. Once you're ready, venture out into the city to begin your exploration of Leipzig's historic heart. Lace up your walking shoes, grab a map or your phone, and get ready to immerse yourself in the sights, sounds, and flavors of this dynamic city.

Midday: Old Town Exploration
Your first stop of the day is the charming Old Town, where centuries of history come to life in its cobblestone streets and medieval architecture. Begin your exploration at the Marktplatz, the bustling

heart of the Old Town, where the iconic Altes Rathaus (Old Town Hall) and Alte Börse (Old Stock Exchange) stand as silent witnesses to Leipzig's past. Stroll through the Markt, where vendors sell fresh produce, flowers, and souvenirs, and take in the sights and sounds of daily life in Leipzig. Don't miss the chance to step inside the historic Nikolaikirche (St. Nicholas Church), where peaceful tranquility awaits amidst the bustling city streets.

Afternoon: Cultural Immersion

After a leisurely morning exploring the Old Town, it's time to delve deeper into Leipzig's rich cultural heritage at its renowned museums and galleries. Make your way to the Museum of Fine Arts, home to an impressive collection of European art spanning from the Middle Ages to the present day. Admire masterpieces by renowned artists such as Lucas Cranach the Elder, Caspar David Friedrich, and Auguste Rodin as you wander through the museum's galleries. Next, head to the Grassi Museum Complex, where three museums await to captivate your imagination. Explore the Museum of Applied Arts, where exquisite porcelain, textiles, and decorative arts showcase Leipzig's craftsmanship and creativity. Then, venture into the Museum of Ethnography to discover artifacts and treasures from around the world, offering insight into diverse cultures and traditions. Finally, visit the Museum of Musical Instruments to marvel at its vast collection of instruments from different periods and regions, each with its own unique story to tell.

Evening: Dinner and Reflection

As the day draws to a close, treat yourself to a well-deserved dinner at one of Leipzig's charming restaurants or cafes. Whether you're craving traditional German cuisine, international flavors, or something more exotic, Leipzig's culinary scene offers something for every palate. As you savor your meal and reflect on the day's adventures, take a moment to appreciate the beauty and wonder of Leipzig. From its historic landmarks and cultural treasures to its warm hospitality and vibrant atmosphere, Leipzig has captured your heart from the very beginning, promising even more excitement and discovery in the days to come.

Day 1 in Leipzig has been a journey of arrival and discovery, filled with memorable experiences and enchanting moments. From exploring the historic Old Town to immersing yourself in the city's cultural riches, you've only just scratched the surface of all that Leipzig has to offer. As you retire for the night, filled with anticipation for the adventures that await, remember that the best is yet to come in this captivating city. So rest well, dear traveler, for tomorrow brings another day of exploration and wonder in the enchanting city of Leipzig.

Day 2
Musical Heritage and Cultural Exploration

Today promises to be another day filled with discovery, as you delve deeper into the city's rich musical heritage and cultural treasures. From exploring historic landmarks to immersing yourself in the sights and sounds of Leipzig's vibrant arts scene, get ready for a day of exploration and inspiration.

Morning: Bach's Legacy

Start your day with a journey into the heart of Leipzig's musical heritage at the St. Thomas Church (Thomaskirche). As you step inside this historic church, you'll be transported back in time to the era of Johann Sebastian Bach, who served as the church's Kapellmeister for 27 years. Take a moment to admire the beautiful interior, with its ornate altar and soaring ceilings, before making your way to Bach's final resting place in the chancel.

If you're lucky, you may have the chance to attend the morning service and experience the world-famous Thomanerchor (St. Thomas Boys Choir) in action. Listen as their angelic voices fill the church with music, creating a truly magical and unforgettable experience.

After your visit to the St. Thomas Church, take a leisurely stroll through the surrounding streets, where you'll find charming cafes, boutiques, and galleries waiting to be discovered. Be sure to stop by the Bach Museum, located just a short walk from the church, to learn more about the life and work of Leipzig's most famous composer through interactive exhibits and multimedia installations.

Afternoon: Musical Heritage Trail

Continue your exploration of Leipzig's musical heritage with a walk along the Musikalischer Bachweg (Musical Bach Trail). This scenic route traces Bach's footsteps through the city's streets and squares, allowing you to follow in the footsteps of the great composer and discover the places where he lived, worked, and performed. As you wander along the trail, keep an eye out for landmarks such as the Thomaskirchhof, where Bach's statue stands proudly in front of the St. Thomas Church, and the Bach Monument in the Rosental Park, a tribute to the composer's enduring legacy. Take your time to soak in the sights and sounds of Leipzig's musical history, pausing to reflect on the profound impact that Bach's music has had on the world.

Evening: Classical Concert

End your day on a high note with a classical concert at one of Leipzig's renowned music venues. Whether you prefer chamber music, orchestral performances, or solo recitals, Leipzig offers a wealth of options for classical music enthusiasts to enjoy. Head to the Gewandhaus, home to the Leipzig Gewandhaus Orchestra, one of the oldest and most prestigious orchestras in the world. Sit back, relax, and let the music wash over you as you experience the timeless beauty and elegance of classical music in this historic concert hall.

Alternatively, venture to one of Leipzig's beautiful churches or cathedrals, where you can enjoy a performance of sacred music in a breathtaking setting. From Bach's cantatas to Handel's oratorios, Leipzig's churches offer a truly transcendent musical experience that will leave you feeling uplifted and inspired. As the final notes fade away and the concert comes to a close, take a moment to reflect on the day's adventures and the beauty of Leipzig's musical heritage. Tomorrow promises another day of exploration and discovery in this enchanting city, so rest up and get ready for more unforgettable experiences to come.

Day 3
Exploring Leipzig's Creative Side

Greetings on Day 3 of your journey in Leipzig! Today is all about discovering the creative energy that permeates the city's streets and immersing yourself in its thriving arts scene. Prepare yourself for a day full of inspiration, adventure, and artistic discovery as you visit street art hotspots and modern art galleries.

Morning: Artistic Enclaves

Kick off your day with a visit to one of Leipzig's creative hubs, the Spinnerei. This former cotton mill has been transformed into a sprawling complex of artist studios, galleries, and exhibition spaces, making it the perfect place to immerse yourself in Leipzig's contemporary art scene. Take a leisurely stroll through the Spinnerei's industrial-chic surroundings, stopping to explore the various galleries and studios that call this creative enclave home. From paintings and sculptures to photography and multimedia installations, the Spinnerei offers a diverse array of artistic experiences to enjoy.

Be sure to visit the Spinnerei's onsite shops and boutiques, where you can browse for unique souvenirs and gifts crafted by local artists and designers. Whether you're looking for handmade jewelry, screen-printed textiles, or limited-edition prints, you're sure to find something special to take home with you.

Afternoon: Street Art Safari

After a morning of exploring Leipzig's contemporary art scene, venture out into the city to discover its vibrant street art scene. Leipzig is home to a thriving community of street artists, whose colorful murals, graffiti, and installations adorn buildings and walls throughout the city.

Join a guided street art tour or simply wander at your own pace, keeping an eye out for hidden gems and striking works of art. From large-scale murals in the Plagwitz and Connewitz neighborhoods to hidden alleyways and abandoned buildings, Leipzig offers endless opportunities for street art enthusiasts to explore and discover. As you wander through the streets, take the time to appreciate the creativity and talent of Leipzig's street artists, whose work reflects the city's dynamic culture and diverse communities. Snap photos of your favorite pieces and share them with friends and fellow travelers, spreading the beauty and inspiration of Leipzig's street art scene far and wide.

Evening: Alternative Scene

As night falls, dive into Leipzig's alternative scene with a visit to its eclectic bars, cafes, and clubs. From underground music venues to bohemian hangouts, Leipzig offers plenty of options for an unforgettable night out.

Head to the Karl-Liebknecht-Straße, known locally as "KarLi," where you'll find a lively mix of bars, cafes, and restaurants catering to Leipzig's alternative crowd. Grab a drink at a cozy pub or beer garden, then dance the night away at one of the street's many clubs and live music venues.

Alternatively, explore Leipzig's vibrant alternative scene in the Plagwitz and Connewitz neighborhoods, where you'll find an array of bars, clubs, and cultural spaces tucked away in historic industrial buildings and former factories. Whether you're into punk, indie, electronic, or experimental music, Leipzig's alternative scene has something for everyone to enjoy. As you soak in the sights and sounds of Leipzig's alternative nightlife, take a moment to appreciate the city's creative energy and free-spirited atmosphere. Tomorrow promises another day of adventure and discovery in this dynamic and diverse city, so savor every moment of your Leipzig experience.

Day 4
Nature and Relaxation

This is Day 4 of your Leipzig adventure! Today is all about escaping the hustle and bustle of the city and reconnecting with nature in Leipzig's beautiful green spaces. From tranquil forests to botanical gardens, get ready for a day of relaxation, rejuvenation, and outdoor adventure.

Morning: Escape to the Outdoors
Start your day by leaving the city behind and venturing into Leipzig's lush greenery. Head to the Leipzig Riverside Forest (Leipziger Auwald), a sprawling nature reserve that stretches along the banks of the White Elster, Pleiße, and Parthe rivers. Lace up your hiking boots or rent a bike, and set out to explore the forest's scenic trails and peaceful pathways.

As you wander through the forest, keep an eye out for native wildlife such as deer, foxes, and birds, and take in the sights and sounds of nature all around you. Stop by one of the forest's tranquil lakes or ponds for a moment of quiet reflection, or simply bask in the beauty of Leipzig's natural landscape.

Afternoon: Botanical Bliss

After a morning of outdoor exploration, make your way to the Leipzig Botanical Garden (Leipziger Botanische Garten) for an afternoon of botanical bliss. Spread across 10 hectares, this stunning garden is home to over 7,000 species of plants from around the world, making it the perfect place to immerse yourself in nature's beauty.

Take a leisurely stroll through the garden's themed sections, from the tropical rainforest to the desert oasis, and marvel at the diversity of plant life on display. Admire exotic flowers, towering trees, and rare species, and breathe in the fragrant scents of the garden as you wander through its pathways and greenhouses. Be sure to visit the Botanical Garden's highlight attractions, such as the Palm House, with its impressive collection of tropical plants, and the Chinese Garden, a tranquil retreat inspired by traditional Chinese landscapes. Don't forget to bring your camera to capture the garden's stunning vistas and botanical wonders.

Evening: Sunset Serenity

As the day draws to a close, wind down with a leisurely stroll along the Karl-Heine-Kanal, a picturesque waterway that winds its way through Leipzig's Plagwitz neighborhood. Watch as the setting sun casts a golden glow over the canal, painting the sky in hues of orange and pink.

Stop at one of the canal-side cafes or beer gardens to enjoy a refreshing drink or a delicious meal as you take in the sunset views. Listen to the gentle lapping of the water against the shore and the distant hum of city life, and savor the peace and serenity of this idyllic setting. As you reflect on the day's adventures and the beauty of Leipzig's natural landscape, feel a sense of gratitude for the opportunity to experience such tranquility and beauty in the heart of the city. Tomorrow promises another day of exploration and discovery in Leipzig, but for now, simply enjoy the moment and let the beauty of the sunset wash over you.

Day 5
Culinary Delights

Welcome to your journey across Leipzig on Day 5! Today is all about discovering the city's unique food scene and treating your senses to some indulgence. A day full of culinary discoveries and delights awaits you, from classic German fare to flavors from around the world.

Morning: Market Exploration
Start your day with a visit to one of Leipzig's bustling markets, where you can immerse yourself in the sights, sounds, and flavors of the city. Head to the Leipzig Farmers' Market (Leipziger Bauernmarkt) at the Leipzig Hauptbahnhof, where local farmers and producers gather to sell their fresh produce, meats, cheeses, and baked goods.

Take your time to wander through the market stalls, sampling seasonal fruits and vegetables, artisanal cheeses, and freshly baked bread. Chat with the vendors and learn about their products and practices, gaining insight into Leipzig's vibrant food culture and culinary traditions.

Afternoon: Culinary Adventures

After exploring the market, embark on a culinary journey through Leipzig's diverse food scene. Whether you're craving traditional German dishes or international flavors, Leipzig offers a wide range of options to satisfy every palate.

Head to a local restaurant or bistro to indulge in a hearty lunch of German classics such as schnitzel, bratwurst, or sauerbraten. Pair your meal with a crisp local beer or a glass of refreshing Riesling, and savor the flavors of Leipzig's rich culinary heritage.

Alternatively, explore Leipzig's street food scene for a taste of global flavors from around the world. From Vietnamese pho and Middle Eastern falafel to Mexican tacos and Korean bibimbap, Leipzig's food trucks and market stalls offer a tantalizing array of options for adventurous eaters.

Evening: Dining Delights

As night falls, treat yourself to a memorable dinner at one of Leipzig's top-rated restaurants, where talented chefs showcase the best of local and seasonal ingredients in creative and delicious dishes. Whether you prefer fine dining or cozy comfort food, Leipzig's culinary scene promises an unforgettable dining experience.

Choose from a range of restaurants serving up innovative cuisine inspired by Leipzig's diverse culinary traditions, from modern interpretations of classic dishes to inventive fusion fare. Sit back, relax, and enjoy a leisurely meal with friends or loved ones, soaking in the ambiance and savoring every bite.

After dinner, why not take a leisurely stroll through Leipzig's streets, enjoying the city's illuminated landmarks and vibrant nightlife? Whether you choose to continue your culinary adventure with a nightcap at a cozy bar or simply wander and take in the sights, Leipzig offers endless opportunities for relaxation and enjoyment after dark.

As you reflect on the day's culinary delights and the flavors of Leipzig's vibrant food scene, feel a sense of satisfaction and contentment knowing that you've experienced the best that the city has to offer. Tomorrow promises another day of exploration and discovery, but for now, let yourself be swept away by the pleasures of good food, good company, and good times in Leipzig.

Day 6
Day Trip Excursion

Greetings on your sixth day of exploration in Leipzig! For an interesting day trip excursion to one of the neighboring attractions, we're leaving the city limits today. Leipzig and its surroundings provide a plethora of options for exploration and discovery, regardless of your interests in history, culture, or outdoor activities.

Morning: Journey Beyond Leipzig

After a leisurely breakfast, it's time to hit the road and journey beyond Leipzig to your chosen destination. Whether you're traveling by car, train, or organized tour, the journey itself promises to be part of the adventure, offering scenic views of the countryside and glimpses of life outside the city.

If you're in the mood for history and culture, consider visiting the nearby city of Dresden, known for its stunning architecture, rich cultural heritage, and fascinating history. Marvel at the iconic Frauenkirche, explore the historic Altstadt (Old Town), and stroll along the picturesque banks of the Elbe River as you soak in the beauty and charm of this enchanting city.

Alternatively, if you're craving outdoor adventure and natural beauty, head to the Saxon Switzerland National Park, a rugged landscape of sandstone cliffs, deep gorges, and dense forests. Lace up your hiking boots and hit the trails to explore this breathtaking wilderness, taking in panoramic views of the Elbe River Valley and discovering hidden gems around every corner.

Afternoon: Sightseeing and Exploration
Spend the afternoon exploring your chosen destination, whether it's Dresden's historic landmarks or the natural wonders of Saxon Switzerland. Take a guided tour to learn about the area's history, culture, and ecology, or venture out on your own to discover hidden gems and off-the-beaten-path attractions. In Dresden, be sure to visit the Zwinger Palace, home to a world-class collection of art and artifacts, and the Semperoper, one of Europe's most prestigious opera houses. Take a leisurely stroll along the Brühl's Terrace, known as the "Balcony of Europe," and enjoy panoramic views of the city and the Elbe River.

In Saxon Switzerland, challenge yourself with a hike to the Bastei Bridge, a spectacular rock formation that offers breathtaking views of the surrounding landscape. Explore the picturesque town of Rathen, nestled in the heart of the national park, and discover charming cafes, shops, and viewpoints along the way.

Evening: Return to Leipzig

As the day comes to a close, it's time to bid farewell to your day trip destination and return to Leipzig. Whether you're traveling by car, train, or bus, take the opportunity to relax and reflect on the day's adventures as you make your way back to the city.

As you arrive back in Leipzig, take a moment to appreciate the comfort and familiarity of the city's streets and landmarks. Whether you're returning to your accommodation or heading out for dinner and drinks, Leipzig welcomes you with open arms, ready to embrace you once again in its warm hospitality and vibrant energy. As you reflect on the day's excursions and the memories you've made, feel a sense of gratitude for the opportunity to explore beyond the confines of the city and discover the beauty and diversity of the surrounding region. Tomorrow promises another day of adventure and discovery in Leipzig, but for now, take a moment to rest and recharge, knowing that you've made the most of your day trip excursion and experienced the best that the region has to offer.

Day 7
Farewell Leipzig

The last day of your trip around Leipzig is here: Day 7. Leipzig is a charming city, so even though it's always difficult to say goodbye, now is the perfect time to cherish every second and make the most of your remaining time here.

Morning: Last-Minute Explorations
Begin your day with some last-minute explorations of Leipzig's streets and squares. Take a leisurely stroll through the city center, soaking in the sights and sounds of Leipzig's bustling streets and historic landmarks. Visit any attractions or landmarks you may have missed during your stay, or simply wander and take in the beauty of the city one last time.

Stop by a local bakery or cafe to pick up a delicious breakfast or snack to enjoy on the go, and take the opportunity to chat with locals and fellow travelers as you navigate Leipzig's charming streets. Whether you're exploring solo or with friends, savor every moment of your final morning in Leipzig, knowing that you've experienced the best that the city has to offer.

Afternoon: Souvenir Shopping

No trip to Leipzig would be complete without picking up some souvenirs and mementos to remember your time in the city. Spend the afternoon exploring Leipzig's shops and boutiques, where you'll find a treasure trove of unique gifts, crafts, and keepsakes to take home with you.

Head to the city center to browse for souvenirs at Leipzig's historic markets and artisanal shops, where you'll find everything from handmade crafts and local delicacies to traditional German gifts and souvenirs. Whether you're looking for a piece of Leipzig's musical heritage, a taste of its culinary delights, or a reminder of its rich history and culture, Leipzig offers plenty of options for meaningful and memorable souvenirs.

Evening: Reflection and Departure

As the sun sets on your Leipzig adventure, take a moment to reflect on the memories you've made and the experiences you've shared during your time in the city. Gather with friends or loved ones for a final dinner together, where you can reminisce about your favorite moments and toast to new adventures on the horizon. As you prepare to depart Leipzig and return home or continue your travels, take one last look around and soak in the sights and sounds of the city. Whether it's the majestic architecture of the Old Town, the vibrant energy of the streets, or the warm hospitality of the locals, Leipzig has left its mark on you in more ways than one. As you bid farewell to Leipzig and make your way to the airport, train station, or bus terminal, carry with you the memories of your time in this enchanting city. Know that Leipzig will always hold a special place in your heart as a city of discovery, adventure, and endless possibilities. Until next time, farewell Leipzig, and may your travels bring you back to this vibrant city again soon.

CHAPTER 8
PRACTICAL INFORMATION AND
TIPS

Etiquette and Customs in Leipzig

Leipzig is a place where tradition and modernity blend seamlessly. Understanding the etiquette and customs of Leipzig will not only help you feel more at home but also ensure you make a positive impression on the locals. This chapter will guide you through the essential aspects of social norms, dining etiquette, business conduct, and local customs in Leipzig.

In Leipzig, as in the rest of Germany, greetings are an essential part of daily interactions. A polite greeting sets a positive tone for any encounter. When meeting someone for the first time, a firm handshake, direct eye contact, and a friendly smile are standard. It's customary to say "Guten Tag" (Good day) or "Hallo" (Hello). For more formal occasions, use "Guten Morgen" (Good morning) or "Guten Abend" (Good evening).

Germans, including those in Leipzig, appreciate a respectful approach in conversation. Initially, use the formal "Sie" (you) when addressing someone you don't know well or in a professional setting. Switching to the informal "du" (you) usually happens by mutual agreement, and the transition might be accompanied by a brief clinking of glasses or a shared moment, often signaled by one person suggesting it: "Wir können uns duzen?" (Shall we use du?). Unlike some cultures where cheek-kissing is common, Leipzig residents generally prefer less physical contact when greeting, especially in formal settings. A handshake suffices in most cases. Among close friends and family, a hug or a quick kiss on the cheek might be appropriate, but it's best to let the locals initiate such gestures.

2. Dining Etiquette

Table Manners

Dining in Leipzig can be a delightful experience, enriched by understanding the local table manners. When invited to a meal, whether at a restaurant or someone's home, arrive on time as punctuality is valued. Before starting to eat, wait for the host or the oldest person to say "Guten Appetit" (Enjoy your meal) and then you can begin.

Using Utensils

The European style of using cutlery is prevalent in Leipzig.Grasp the knife with your right hand and the fork with your left. After cutting your food, you typically keep the fork in your left hand to eat. Place your knife and fork parallel on your plate when you are finished, indicating that you have completed your meal.

Toasting

Toasting is a common practice in Leipzig. It's typical to clink glasses with everyone at the table before taking your first sip. This involves making eye contact and exchanging cheers with each other.(Cheers!). If you're not drinking alcohol, it's still polite to join the toast with your non-alcoholic beverage.

Paying the Bill

In restaurants, it's typical to ask for the bill by saying "Die Rechnung, bitte" (The bill, please). When the bill arrives, tipping around 5-10% of the total amount is customary, depending on the level of service. Unlike in some countries, the tip is usually given directly to the server when paying, rather than left on the table.

3. Gift Giving
When to Bring a Gift

Gift-giving in Leipzig follows specific customs. If invited to someone's home, it's polite to bring a small gift. Flowers, a bottle of wine, or chocolates are common and appreciated choices. Ensure that flowers are given in odd numbers (except for twelve) as even numbers are associated with funerals.

Receiving Gifts
When receiving a gift, open it immediately and show appreciation. Even if the gift is modest, expressing gratitude and enthusiasm is considered polite. Compliment the gift and thank the giver sincerely.

4. Cultural Norms and Traditions
Respect for Privacy

Leipzigers value their privacy and personal space. In public places, such as parks or public transport, keep conversations at a moderate volume. Avoiding overly personal questions in initial conversations is also appreciated.

Queuing
Orderliness and patience are hallmarks of Leipzig's public etiquette. When waiting in line, whether at a bus stop, a bakery, or a museum, maintain your place and wait your turn without pushing or cutting in line. This respect for queuing is a reflection of broader societal values of fairness and consideration.

Recycling and Environmental Awareness

Leipzig, like the rest of Germany, is committed to environmental sustainability. Recycling is taken seriously, with separate bins for paper, plastics, glass, and organic waste. Familiarize yourself with the recycling system and dispose of your waste accordingly. Participating in this practice shows respect for local customs and environmental efforts.

5. Workplace Etiquette

Professional Conduct

In the workplace, punctuality and professionalism are highly valued. Meetings typically start on time, and being late can be seen as disrespectful. During meetings, listen attentively, and contribute thoughtfully. Germans appreciate clear, direct communication, so state your points concisely and avoid unnecessary embellishments.

Dress Code

Business attire in Leipzig tends to be conservative, especially in more formal industries like finance or law. Dark suits for men and professional dresses or suits for women are common. In creative industries, the dress code might be more relaxed, but maintaining a neat and presentable appearance is still important.

Work-Life Balance

Leipzigers value a healthy work-life balance. While they work diligently during office hours, evenings and weekends are typically reserved for family, hobbies, and relaxation. Respecting this balance by not contacting colleagues outside of working hours unless absolutely necessary is appreciated.

6. Communication Style
Directness

Leipzigers, like many Germans, are known for their direct communication style. They value honesty and clarity over vagueness or indirectness. While this might initially seem blunt to some, it's important to understand that this directness is not intended to be rude but to ensure effective and transparent communication.

Non-Verbal Cues

Non-verbal communication also plays a significant role. Maintaining eye contact during conversations is seen as a sign of confidence and sincerity. However, avoid prolonged staring, as it can be perceived as intrusive. Gestures should be controlled and purposeful; excessive hand movements or fidgeting can be distracting.

Politeness

Politeness in Leipzig is expressed through actions rather than excessive words. Saying "Bitte" (please) and "Danke" (thank you) in appropriate situations is essential. Holding doors open, offering your seat to someone in need on public transport, and other small acts of kindness are everyday courtesies that make a big difference.

Embracing the etiquette and customs of Leipzig will not only enrich your experience but also endear you to the locals. This city, with its deep historical roots and vibrant contemporary culture, offers a welcoming environment for those who respect and engage with its traditions. By following these guidelines, you'll find that Leipzigers are warm, friendly, and eager to share their unique heritage with you. Enjoy your time in Leipzig, and let these customs guide you in creating meaningful connections and unforgettable memories.

Language and Communication in Leipzig

Leipzig has significant contributions to the fields of language and communication. This chapter delves into the unique aspects of Leipzig's linguistic landscape, examining how its historical evolution, educational institutions, and contemporary cultural dynamics have shaped the way people communicate. We will explore the influence of key historical figures, the role of multilingualism, and the impact of digital communication in modern Leipzig. By understanding these elements, we gain a comprehensive view of how language and communication intersect in this fascinating city.

Languages Spoken in Leipzig

While German is the predominant language in Leipzig, the city's multicultural population means that many other languages are spoken as well. Turkish, Arabic, Russian, Polish, and Vietnamese are among the most common, reflecting the city's diverse immigrant communities. Additionally, English is widely used, particularly in academic and business settings, underscoring Leipzig's global connections.

Cultural Exchanges and Multilingualism

Multilingualism in Leipzig facilitates rich cultural exchanges, enhancing the city's vibrant cultural scene. Festivals, cultural events, and community organizations celebrate the linguistic and cultural diversity of the city's inhabitants. For example, the annual "Leipziger Buchmesse" (Leipzig Book Fair) is not only a significant literary event but also a celebration of multilingualism, featuring authors and publishers from around the world. Such events provide opportunities for intercultural dialogue and promote the appreciation of different languages and cultures.

Digital Innovation and Startups

Leipzig has emerged as a hub for digital innovation and startups, with many companies focusing on language technology and communication tools. For instance, several local startups are developing applications for language learning, translation, and speech recognition, contributing to the city's reputation as a center for technological advancement in language services. These innovations are not only enhancing communication within Leipzig but also connecting the city to global markets.

Language, Identity, and Community

Language is a crucial component of identity and community in Leipzig. The way people speak and the languages they use are integral to their sense of self and belonging. This section examines the relationship between language and identity in Leipzig, exploring how linguistic diversity shapes community life.

Language and Regional Identity

Leipzigers often take pride in their regional dialect, known as "Sächsisch" or Saxon dialect. This dialect, characterized by distinct pronunciation and vocabulary, is an important marker of local identity. While standard German is used in formal settings, many residents use Sächsisch in everyday conversations, reinforcing their connection to the region's cultural heritage. The dialect is also celebrated in local literature, music, and theater, highlighting its role in the city's cultural expression.

Language and Immigrant Communities

For immigrant communities in Leipzig, language plays a key role in maintaining cultural ties and facilitating integration. Community centers and cultural organizations offer language courses and support services, helping newcomers learn German while preserving their native languages. This bilingual approach enables immigrants to participate fully in Leipzig's social and economic life while retaining their cultural identities.

Language proficiency is crucial for social integration in Leipzig. The ability to communicate effectively in German opens up opportunities for education, employment, and civic participation. The city offers numerous programs to support language learning, including free or subsidized German courses for immigrants and refugees. These initiatives aim to promote inclusivity and ensure that all residents can contribute to and benefit from the city's development.

Language and communication are central to the life and identity of Leipzig. From its historical roots as a multilingual trade hub to its modern role as a center for linguistic research and digital innovation, the city exemplifies the dynamic interplay of language and culture. The rich linguistic diversity of Leipzig's population, the contributions of its educational institutions, and the influence of digital communication all shape the way people connect and interact. By understanding these elements, we gain a deeper appreciation of how language and communication continue to evolve in this vibrant city, enriching its cultural fabric and fostering a sense of community.

In summary, Leipzig's linguistic landscape is a testament to its history, its people, and its future. As the city continues to grow and change, its commitment to embracing linguistic diversity and fostering effective communication will remain a cornerstone of its identity.

Simple Language Phrases to Know (in Different Categories)

Leipzig is an exciting destination for travelers. While many people in Leipzig speak English, knowing a few key phrases in German can enhance your experience, making it easier to connect with locals and navigate the city. This chapter will guide you through simple language phrases categorized for various situations you might encounter in Leipzig. Whether you're ordering food, asking for directions, or engaging in small talk, these phrases will help you feel more confident and integrated during your stay.

Asking for Directions

Navigating a new city can be challenging, but these phrases will help you find your way around Leipzig more easily.

Wo ist ...? (Where is ...?)
Wie komme ich zum ...? (How do I get to ...?)
Links (Left)
Rechts (Right)
Geradeaus (Straight ahead)
In der Nähe von . (Near ...)
Entfernt von ...(Far from ...)
Können Sie mir helfen? (Can you help me?)
Ich habe mich verlaufen. (I'm lost.)
Wie weit ist es? (How far is it?)

Dining and Food

Leipzig has a vibrant culinary scene. Whether you're dining out or grabbing a quick bite, these phrases will make ordering food a breeze.

Ich hätte gerne ... (I would like ...)
Die Speisekarte, bitte. (The menu, please.)
Was empfehlen Sie? (What do you recommend?)
Ich bin Vegetarier(in). (I'm a vegetarian.)
Ich habe eine Allergie gegen ... (I'm allergic to ...)
Das schmeckt sehr gut! (That tastes very good!)
Könnte ich die Rechnung bekommen, bitte? (Could I get the bill, please?)
Stilles Wasser (Still water)
Mit Sprudel (Sparkling water)
Zum Hieressen oder zum Mitnehmen? (For here or to go?)

Shopping

Exploring local markets and shops is a delightful way to experience Leipzig. These phrases will help you communicate with shopkeepers and find what you need. Wie viel kostet das?(How much does this cost?)

Kann ich das anprobieren?(Can I try this on?)
Haben Sie das in einer anderen Größe/Farbe? (Do you have this in another size/color?)
Ich nehme es. (I'll take it.)
Ich schaue nur. (I'm just looking.)
Können Sie mir helfen? (Can you help me?)
Könnte ich eine Tüte bekommen, bitte?(Could I get a bag, please?)

Transportation
Getting around Leipzig is straightforward, especially with public transportation. Here are some phrases to help you navigate buses, trams, and trains.

Wo ist die nächste Haltestelle? (Where is the nearest stop?)
Wann kommt der nächste Bus? (When does the next bus arrive?)
Einmal zum Hauptbahnhof, bitte. (One ticket to the main train station, please.)
Wie viel kostet eine Fahrkarte? (How much does a ticket cost?)
Ich möchte ein Tagesticket. (I would like a day ticket.)
Muss ich umsteigen? (Do I need to change/transfer?)
Welche Linie fährt zum ...?(Which line goes to ...?)

Socializing and Small Talk

Engaging with locals can be one of the most rewarding parts of your trip. Use these phrases to start conversations and make friends.

Wie heißen Sie? (What's your name?)
Ich heiße ...(My name is ...)
Woher kommen Sie? (Where are you from?)
Ich komme aus ... (I'm from ...)
Was machen Sie beruflich?(What do you do for a living?)
Haben Sie Hobbys? (Do you have hobbies?)
Was sind Ihre Lieblingsplätze in Leipzig? (What are your favorite places in Leipzig?)
Es freut mich, Sie kennenzulernen. (Nice to meet you.)

Accommodations

Communicating with hotel staff or landlords can ensure a comfortable stay. These phrases will help you address your needs and preferences.
Ich habe eine Reservierung. (I have a reservation.)
Haben Sie ein Zimmer frei? (Do you have a room available?)

Wie viel kostet ein Zimmer pro Nacht? (How much is a room per night?)
Gibt es WLAN? (Is there Wi-Fi?)
Ich brauche frische Handtücher. (I need fresh towels.)
Können Sie mir ein Taxi rufen? (Can you call a taxi for me?)
Wo ist das Frühstückszimmer? (Where is the breakfast room?)

Health and Safety Tips

Leipzig offers a rich blend of history, culture, and modern amenities. Whether you're a resident or a visitor, ensuring your health and safety while enjoying all that Leipzig has to offer is paramount. This chapter provides comprehensive tips to help you stay healthy and safe, making your time in this beautiful city as enjoyable and worry-free as possible.

Leipzig is generally a safe city, but like any urban area, it's essential to stay vigilant and take common-sense precautions.

1. Stay Aware of Your Surroundings: Whether you're exploring the bustling city center or the quieter suburbs, always be mindful of your surroundings. Avoid walking alone in poorly lit or unfamiliar areas at night.

2. Emergency Numbers: Familiarize yourself with the local emergency numbers. In Germany, dial 112 for medical emergencies and fire services, and 110 for the police.

3. Keep Valuables Secure: Petty theft can occur, especially in crowded areas like public transportation and popular tourist spots. Use a money belt or a secure bag to keep your valuables close and avoid displaying expensive items.

4. Transportation Safety: Leipzig boasts an efficient public transportation system, including trams, buses, and trains. Ensure you buy a valid ticket to avoid fines, and always stay behind the safety lines on platforms. Maintaining your health while in Leipzig involves staying informed about local healthcare options, staying hydrated, and ensuring you have access to necessary medications and services.

1. Healthcare Facilities: Leipzig has numerous hospitals and clinics providing excellent healthcare services. The University Hospital Leipzig (Universitätsklinikum Leipzig) is one of the leading medical centers. In case of non-emergency health issues, pharmacies (Apotheken) are readily available throughout the city.

2. Health Insurance: Make sure you have adequate health insurance coverage. EU residents can use their European Health Insurance Card (EHIC) for medical services. Non-EU visitors should ensure their travel insurance covers medical expenses in Germany.

3. Stay Hydrated and Eat Well:Drink plenty of water, especially during the warmer months. Leipzig has clean tap water that is safe to drink. Enjoy the local cuisine but maintain a balanced diet to keep your energy levels up.

4. Exercise Regularly: Leipzig offers numerous parks and green spaces, such as Clara-Zetkin Park and the Leipzig Riverside Forest, perfect for jogging, walking, or cycling. Regular exercise helps maintain physical and mental health.

5. Mental Health: If you find yourself feeling overwhelmed or anxious, don't hesitate to seek help. There are several counseling services available, including English-speaking therapists.

Safety in Daily Activities
Whether you're commuting, shopping, or enjoying leisure activities, following these safety tips will help ensure your well-being.

1. Commuting Safely
Cycling: Leipzig is a bike-friendly city with numerous cycling paths. Always wear a helmet, follow traffic rules, and use lights at night.
  Public Transport: Use well-lit and busy tram stops and stations, especially at night.Watch out for your possessions and stay away from those who seem fishy.

2. Shopping: When visiting markets like the Leipzig Christmas Market or shopping malls like Höfe am Brühl, stay aware of your surroundings. Keep your wallet and personal items secure, and be cautious of pickpockets in crowded areas.

3. Leisure Activities: Whether you're visiting museums, attending concerts, or enjoying the nightlife, always have a plan for getting home safely. Use reputable taxi services or public transportation, and avoid accepting rides from strangers.

Special Tips for Families
Families with children need to take additional precautions to ensure everyone's safety and enjoyment.

1. Child Safety: Teach your children about the importance of staying close in crowded places. Equip them with a card containing your contact information in case they get lost.

2. Family-Friendly Activities: Leipzig offers numerous family-friendly attractions such as the Leipzig Zoo and the Belantis amusement park. Ensure your children are supervised at all times and aware of emergency procedures.

3. Healthcare for Children: Keep a list of pediatricians and the nearest hospitals with pediatric services. Ensure your children are up-to-date with vaccinations and carry a basic first aid kit for minor injuries.

Staying Safe Outdoors

Leipzig's beautiful parks, lakes, and recreational areas provide ample opportunities for outdoor activities. Use these safety advice when taking in the scenery.

1. Weather Awareness: Leipzig experiences varied weather conditions.Before you go outside, check the weather forecast and make sure you are dressed properly. In summer, protect yourself from the sun with sunscreen and hats; in winter, wear layers to stay warm.

2. Swimming Safety: If you plan to swim in local lakes or pools, always follow safety guidelines. Don't swim by yourself; instead, swim in approved places. Pay attention to lifeguard instructions and water conditions.

3. Hiking and Biking: When hiking or biking in areas like the Leipzig Riverside Forest, stay on marked trails, carry a map, and inform someone of your plans. Bring enough water and snacks, and be aware of local wildlife.

Leipzig is a city full of life and opportunities, offering a rich tapestry of experiences for residents and visitors alike. By following these health and safety tips, you can ensure that your time in Leipzig is enjoyable and secure. Stay aware, stay prepared, and immerse yourself in everything this remarkable city has to offer. Remember, your health and safety are paramount, and taking simple, proactive steps can help you make the most of your Leipzig adventure.

Emergency Contacts

In any situation, being prepared with the right emergency contacts can be crucial. Whether you're facing a minor inconvenience or a major emergency, knowing who to call and having their information readily available can make all the difference. This chapter provides a comprehensive list of essential emergency contacts in Leipzig, ensuring you have access to the support and services you need at a moment's notice.

Essential Emergency Numbers

1. Police: 110

The primary contact for any criminal activity, including theft, assault, or any situation where you feel threatened.

2. Fire and Medical Emergency: 112

Use this number for medical emergencies, fires, and urgent situations requiring an ambulance or fire brigade.

24-Hour Taxis
1. Leipzig Taxi Service
 Phone: +49 341 4884
Services: Reliable 24-hour taxi service for safe transportation throughout the city.

Helplines and Hotlines

1. Poison Control Center (Giftnotruf)
Phone: +49 30 19240
Services: Immediate assistance and information in cases of poisoning.

2. Domestic Violence Helpline (Hilfetelefon Gewalt gegen Frauen)
Phone: 08000 116 016
Services: Confidential support for victims of domestic violence, available 24/7.

Having a list of emergency contacts at your fingertips is an essential part of staying safe and secure in Leipzig. Whether you're dealing with a minor issue or a significant emergency, knowing who to call can provide peace of mind and ensure you get the help you need promptly. Keep this list handy and share it with friends or family who might be staying with you or visiting. Your safety is paramount, and being prepared is the first step in ensuring your well-being in this dynamic city.

Communication and Internet Access

Staying connected in Leipzig, whether for personal, business, or emergency purposes, is crucial. This chapter covers everything you need to know about communication and internet access in Leipzig, including mobile services, internet providers, public Wi-Fi, and useful tips for staying connected effortlessly.

Mobile Services

Germany offers a variety of mobile service providers with extensive coverage in Leipzig.
What you should know to get started is as follows:

1. Major Mobile Providers

Deutsche Telekom (T-Mobile) Known for excellent coverage and reliable service.
Vodafone: Offers competitive pricing and strong network coverage.
O2: Provides affordable plans and wide coverage, particularly popular among students and young professionals.

2. Getting a SIM Card

Purchasing: SIM cards can be purchased at airports, convenience stores, electronic shops, and mobile provider stores. Popular locations include Saturn and MediaMarkt.

Registration: Due to German regulations, you must register your SIM card with a valid ID (passport or residence permit) before activation.

3. Prepaid vs. Contract Plans

Prepaid Plans: Ideal for short-term visitors, offering flexibility without long-term commitment. Look for options with data packages to suit your needs.

Contract Plans: Suitable for long-term residents, often including better rates for data, calls, and international usage. Contracts typically range from 12 to 24 months.

4. Top-Up Options

Online: Most providers offer online top-up services via their websites or mobile apps. In-Store: Top-up vouchers can be purchased at various retail locations such as supermarkets, kiosks, and gas stations.

Internet Providers

Leipzig boasts a range of internet service providers (ISPs) offering various plans to meet different needs.

1. Major ISPs

Deutsche Telekom: Offers DSL, VDSL, and fiber-optic connections with high-speed internet plans.Vodafone: Provides cable internet and fiber-optic services with competitive pricing and bundled packages.

1&1: Known for a variety of DSL and VDSL plans with flexible terms. PYUR: Offers cable and fiber-optic internet with affordable plans and bundled options including TV and phone services.

2. Choosing the Right Plan

Speed Requirements: Determine your internet speed needs based on usage. Basic browsing and streaming may only require lower speeds, while gaming or heavy downloading benefits from higher speeds.

Bundled Services: Consider bundles that include TV, phone, and internet for cost savings and convenience.

Contract Length: Most ISPs offer contracts ranging from 12 to 24 months. Shorter-term options may be available but often at higher rates.

Useful Apps, Websites, and Maps

Navigating Leipzig effectively requires the right tools to make your experience as smooth and enjoyable as possible. This chapter provides a curated list of essential apps, websites, and maps that will help you with everything from transportation and dining to sightseeing and local services. These resources are designed to enhance your stay, whether you are a visitor or a resident.

Essential Apps
1. Transportation and Navigation

DB Navigator: This app from Deutsche Bahn is essential for train travel across Germany. It provides schedules, ticket booking, and real-time updates.

LeipzigMOVE: The official app for Leipzig's public transportation system, including trams, buses, and bike rentals. It offers route planning, ticket purchasing, and live departure information.

Google Maps: Ideal for general navigation, it includes public transit routes, walking directions, and cycling paths. It also features business information and reviews.

BVG Jelbi: An app for integrated mobility services including ride-sharing, bike rentals, and public transport in and around Leipzig.

2. Accommodation and Dining

Booking.com: A comprehensive app for booking hotels, apartments, and other accommodations. User reviews and detailed descriptions help you choose the best place to stay.

Airbnb: Great for finding unique accommodations, from single rooms to entire homes, often with local hosts offering insider tips.

Yelp: Useful for finding restaurants, cafes, bars, and reviews from other diners. It includes information on opening hours, menus, and contact details.

OpenTable:Allows you to make reservations at a wide range of restaurants in Leipzig, ensuring you get a table at popular spots.

3. Local Information and Events

Leipzig Travel:The official app by Leipzig Tourismus und Marketing GmbH provides detailed information on attractions, events, and tours. It includes a city guide, maps, and a calendar of events. Eventim:This app is essential for purchasing tickets to concerts, theater performances, festivals, and other events in Leipzig.

Meetup:Use this app to find local groups and events based on your interests. It's great for meeting new people and exploring hobbies.

4. Language and Translation

Google Translate: Useful for translating text and speech. The app's camera feature allows you to translate text in images, which is helpful for signs and menus. Duolingo: A fun and interactive way to learn German, or to brush up on your language skills if you already have some knowledge.

CONCLUSION

Leipzig is more than just a city; it's a vibrant tapestry of history, culture, innovation, and community. From its rich musical heritage and stunning architecture to its bustling markets and serene parks, Leipzig offers an experience that is both deeply rooted in tradition and dynamically forward-thinking. This travel guide has provided you with the tools and knowledge to navigate and appreciate the many facets of this remarkable city. As we conclude this journey together, let's reflect on the key aspects that make Leipzig a unique and unforgettable destination, and how you can make the most of your visit.

Leipzig's historical and cultural significance is monumental, particularly in the realms of music and art. The city has been home to some of the most influential composers in history, including Johann Sebastian Bach and Felix Mendelssohn. The Bach Museum and the Mendelssohn House offer a deep dive into their lives and works, allowing you to walk the same streets and inhabit the same spaces that inspired these musical giants.

Leipzig's commitment to the arts is evident in its numerous galleries and museums, such as the Museum of Fine Arts and the Grassi Museum complex. These institutions not only preserve the past but also celebrate contemporary creativity, providing platforms for emerging artists and new art forms. Take the time to immerse yourself in these cultural treasures, as they offer profound insights into the city's soul and its ongoing narrative of artistic expression.

Leipzig is also a city of learning and innovation, with a long-standing tradition of intellectual pursuit. The University of Leipzig, one of the oldest universities in Europe, has been a center of education and research for centuries. Its libraries, lecture halls, and scientific institutes are testament to the city's enduring commitment to knowledge and progress.

Today, Leipzig continues to foster innovation through its vibrant startup scene and cutting-edge research facilities. The city is a hub for technology, media, and creative industries, drawing young professionals and entrepreneurs from around the world. Whether you're visiting as a student, a professional, or an entrepreneur, you'll find a dynamic environment that encourages curiosity and creative thinking.

Leipzig's culinary scene is as diverse as its cultural offerings. Traditional Saxon dishes, such as Sauerbraten and Leipziger Allerlei, provide a taste of the region's rich gastronomic heritage. At the same time, the city's numerous cafes, bistros, and international restaurants reflect its cosmopolitan character. The vibrant Karli Street (Karl-Liebknecht-Straße) is a testament to this, bustling with eateries and bars that cater to every palate and preference.

Don't miss the opportunity to explore the local markets, such as the historic Naschmarkt and the bustling Leipzig Market. These markets offer fresh produce, artisanal goods, and a chance to interact with local vendors and residents. Sampling local specialties and engaging with the culinary scene is a delightful way to experience Leipzig's community spirit and hospitality.

Leipzig is blessed with an abundance of green spaces and natural beauty. The city's parks, such as the expansive Clara Zetkin Park and the tranquil Rosental, provide perfect spots for relaxation and recreation. The Leipzig Riverside Forest (Auwald) offers scenic trails for walking, cycling, and even canoeing, allowing you to escape the urban hustle and connect with nature.

The surrounding region also boasts numerous lakes and waterways, ideal for swimming, boating, and other water sports. Cospudener See and Kulkwitzer See are popular destinations for locals and visitors alike, offering a range of outdoor activities against a backdrop of stunning natural landscapes.

One of the most endearing aspects of Leipzig is its strong sense of community. The city's festivals and events are a testament to this communal spirit, bringing together people from all walks of life in celebration of art, music, food, and more. The Leipzig Bach Festival, the Wave-Gotik-Treffen, and the Leipzig Book Fair are just a few examples of the vibrant events that animate the city throughout the year.

Participating in these festivals provides a unique opportunity to experience the city's culture and traditions firsthand. They also offer a chance to meet new people, forge connections, and create lasting memories. Whether you're dancing to live music, exploring literary works, or simply enjoying the festive atmosphere, these events are integral to the Leipzig experience.

Throughout this guide, we've provided practical information to help you navigate Leipzig with ease. From understanding the public transportation system and finding the best accommodations to knowing where to get medical help and staying connected, these tips are designed to ensure a smooth and enjoyable visit.

Remember to make use of the apps, websites, and maps highlighted in this guide. These tools will help you plan your itinerary, discover hidden gems, and stay informed about local events and services. Whether you're exploring the historic city center, venturing into the surrounding neighborhoods, or taking day trips to nearby attractions, having these resources at your fingertips will enhance your experience.

As you embark on your journey through Leipzig, take the time to immerse yourself fully in the city's rich cultural tapestry. Explore its historical landmarks, savor its culinary delights, engage with its vibrant arts scene, and connect with its welcoming community. Use the knowledge and tips provided in this guide to navigate the city confidently and make the most of every moment.

Leipzig is a city that rewards curiosity and openness. It's a place where past and present converge, where tradition and innovation coexist, and where every street and corner has a story to tell. Whether you're here for a short visit or an extended stay, let the city's spirit inspire you. Discover the hidden treasures, engage with the local culture, and create your own unique Leipzig story.

Leipzig is a city of contrasts and harmonies, a place where history and modernity dance together in a vibrant symphony. It's a city that welcomes you with open arms, invites you to explore its depths, and leaves you with a sense of fulfillment and inspiration. As you leave Leipzig, you take with you not just memories, but a part of its enduring spirit.

We hope this travel guide has equipped you with the insights and tools to experience Leipzig in all its glory. May your journey through this remarkable city be filled with discovery, joy, and meaningful connections. Embrace the adventure, and let Leipzig leave an indelible mark on your heart and soul.

.

Printed in Great Britain
by Amazon

57005075R00126